Structured Mediation in
Divorce Settlement

Structured Mediation in Divorce Settlement

A Handbook for Marital Mediators

O.J. Coogler
Family Mediation Association

Lexington Books
D.C. Heath and Company
Lexington, Massachusetts
Toronto

Library of Congress Cataloging in Publication Data

Coogler, O.J.
   Structured mediation in divorce settlement.

   Bibliography: p. 93
   Includes index.
   1. Divorce—United States. I. Title.
KF535.C66   1978   346'.73'0166   78-4794
ISBN 0-669-02343-4

Third printing, March 1982

Published simultaneously in Canada

Printed in the United States of America

International Standard Book Number: 0-669-02343-4

Library of Congress Catalog Card Number: 78-4794

I am indebted to my former wife and the two attorneys who represented us in our divorce for making me aware of the critical need for a more rational, more civilized way of arranging a parting of the ways. Her life, my life, and our children's lives were unnecessarily embittered by that experience. In my frustration and anger, I kept thinking of something Mahatma Ghandi wrote over half a century ago:

"I have learnt through bitter experience that one supreme lesson, to conserve my anger, and as heat conserved is transmuted into energy, even so our anger can be transmuted into a power which can move the world."

This system of structured mediation is, therefore, my anger transmuted into what I hope is a power to move toward a more humane world for those who find themselves following in my footsteps.

Contents

List of Tables

Preface

When this book was written, the intended readers were to be marital mediators and those who wanted to provide mediation services. However, when a preliminary version of the manuscript appeared as a monograph, it became apparent that it was useful to a much wider audience. Marriage and family counselors, divorce counselors, ministers, family court workers, lawyers, judges, and even couples negotiating divorce settlements have expressed interest. Some family courts have adapted the mediation process to help resolve custody disputes. Lay readers may also find that this book offers much helpful information that is not readily available from other sources.

The book is designed to provide a focal point for marital mediator training programs. However, it cannot be emphasized too strongly that a thorough knowledge of the contents of this book is not sufficient to qualify one for performing mediation services for divorcing couples. Competence as a marital mediator can be developed only by reading the materials listed at the end of each chapter, in addition to personal instruction and supervision.

Since this book is a first effort to describe a new and evolving process, the author welcomes comments and suggestions from readers.

Acknowledgments

Special thanks are due to Martha Kuckleburg for contributing the chapter on tax considerations and to Lynn Carrigan for her research and writing of the chapter on budgeting.

My deep appreciation is expressed to William Neville and Judi Wood, who worked with me in performing mediations under the rules as they were developed, and for their many presentations to professional and civic groups; to Sheila Kessler, who saw mediation as a complement to her work in divorce adjustment; to Morton Deutsch and Kenneth Kressel, who performed the first studies of the effectiveness of mediation, for their many helpful suggestions; to Ruth Weber for her early and continued support of my work; to Peggy Ayers of the Robert Sterling Clark Foundation for her understanding and helpfulness in the first major funding for research and development of structured mediation; to the School of Social Work, University of Georgia, Athens, through whom the Clark Foundation provided support; to Marvin Sussman, Emily Brown, Susan Gettleman, Judi Savage, and Morton and Bernice Hunt for their support and encouragement; to Dorothy Sparer for her brilliant and perceptive editorial assistance; to Lisa Rankin for her flawless typing and attention to detail in preparing the manuscript; to members of the Advisory Board of Directors of the Family Mediation Association; and finally to those many couples who participated in research of their mediation experience.

Appreciation is expressed to the Robert Sterling Clark Foundation of New York for its support of the writing of the monograph upon which this book is based.

A Brief History of Structured Mediation

In the fall of 1974, I began studies that lead to the development of structured mediation. I founded the Family Mediation Association (FMA) as a nonprofit organization in January 1975 and mediated the first divorce settlement through FMA that month. During the next 2½ years, more than a hundred couples participated in the developing program. Since no financial assistance was available, I and two colleagues, William Neville and Judi Wood, contributed our services out of a conviction that structured mediation had important social significance.

These early efforts of the Family Mediation Association were described in talks to many professional, religious, and civic groups. Inquiries about mediation were received from over half the states in the United States and two foreign countries.

In the fall of 1975, Morton Deutsch and Kenneth Kressel were completing a four-year study of resources available to divorcing couples at the Department of Social Psychology, Teachers College, Columbia University. With funds provided by a grant from the Marshall Fund, a pilot study of structured mediation was conducted as a complement to their prior work.

The Family Mediation Association was approached by the Robert Sterling Clark Foundation of New York in the fall of 1976 with an offer of substantial assistance for the further development and research of structured mediation. At the association's suggestion, a grant was made to the School of Social Work, University of Georgia, with Ruth Weber as principal investigator and myself as principal consultant. With assistance from that grant, I wrote a monograph from which the manuscript for this book has been largely derived.

Improving the quality of family life is the continuing goal of the Family Mediation Association. Cooperative methods of conflict resolution can make a major contribution toward this end, especially when the marriage partners divorce. Professional training, certification of competence for using these methods, and consultation for establishing mediation services are now offered by the Family Mediation Association.

1 Why Marital Mediation?

Basic Principles of Mediation

Mediated divorce settlement means resolving the kinds of issues that are involved in dissolving a partnership of any kind. Basically these are

Deciding upon *property* division

Terminating *dependency* upon the relationship

Continuing the *ongoing business* initiated by the partnership

Resolution calls for following a procedure and agreeing upon a value system. The procedure previously followed by most husbands and wives has not worked, and the value system applied has been derived from their respective and usually different role expectations. Often it was a conflict over role expectations which led to the decision to dissolve the marriage in the first place.

On the other hand, when they agree to follow the Marital Mediation Rules, they establish a mutually acceptable value system, called *guidelines,* and an orderly procedural process for reaching settlement.

Marital Mediation Rules

Under the rules,

Property means all the material accumulations made by the couple during the marriage. Each partner is deemed to have contributed and thus has a right to a fair division.

Dependency means that both have established a life-style which includes reliance upon and participation in a relationship that is ending. Though it is both emotional and financial, the rules are designed to deal with the latter.

There is a tendency to think of the wife and the children as the most immediately affected by the financial aspects, so that the financial impact upon the husband is overlooked. How he makes it on what is left for him is regarded as his problem. But in mediation, a major goal is to

1

resolve financial dependency in a way that treats the needs of *all* parties with equal respect and consideration.

The *ongoing business* of a marriage that must continue after divorce is raising the children. How the former marriage partners, who are still parents, will handle this is the final and most important goal of mediation.

What is meant when we speak of mediation, conciliation, and arbitration? How are they used for resolving marital conflicts? How are they different from the approach used by lawyers and the legal system? These are some of the questions that will be briefly answered in the remainder of this chapter and will be dealt with in greater detail in later chapters.

Mediation

When two or more persons are having trouble resolving a controversy, they may agree to turn to a neutral third person who will help them resolve it. Agreeing to work out their problems in this way is called *mediation*. It is also a commitment to reach settlement cooperatively rather than in a competitive struggle with each other.

The role of the neutral third party, or mediator, does not include deciding upon the issues in controversy between the parties. In fact, the mediator must carefully avoid doing so, because making these decisions is the responsibility of the parties. One of the most important advantages of mediation is that the parties are responsible for the decisions reached and are therefore more willing to honor them than when decisions are made by a third party.

Structured Mediation

When a husband and wife agree to reach divorce settlement under the Marital Mediation Rules, they are using a new kind of mediation called structured mediation. In the past, mediation has been conducted without advance agreement upon rules of procedure and guidelines to be followed by the parties and the mediator.

The advantages of structured mediation are the following:

1. The issues to be decided are clearly defined.
2. The issues are limited to those whose resolution is needed for reaching settlement.
3. Procedural methods are established for collecting and examining factual information.

4. All options for settlement of each issue are systematically examined.
5. Options are selected within socially acceptable guidelines.
6. Consequences likely to follow selection of each option are examined.
7. Uninterrupted time for working toward resolution is regularly allocated.
8. Impasses are promptly resolved by arbitration.

Conciliation

Conciliation is another term often used in connection with mediation. The role of the conciliator and of the mediator differ in the following ways:

1. The conciliator offers options for the parties to consider.
2. The conciliator points out advantages and disadvantages of various options.
3. The conciliator encourages the parties to adopt an available option rather than remain at an impasse.

To some extent, the conciliator is taking over the parties' responsibility for examining the issues and discovering options. Conciliation is thus a less desirable procedure than mediation and serves as an alternative to an impasse. It may be needed, not because the parties are unwilling to take responsibility, but because they are often inexperienced in dealing with much of the subject matter.

The stress of underlying emotional issues may also interfere with the couple's ability to reason clearly. A person's accustomed dependency upon a spouse may mask his or her real ability to understand the issues, discover the available options, and rationally consider them.

The mediator must be able to assess all these factors. Doing so calls for a solid background of training and experience in the behavioral sciences. While any one or a combination of these factors may limit a party's ability to function, autonomy and the discovery of personal strengths must be supported at every opportunity. Parties who learn to take responsibility for themselves during mediation are better prepared to handle the demands of postdivorce adjustment.

Arbitration

The arbitrator is also a neutral third party whose role is unlike that of the mediator and conciliator. Arbitration is used to resolve an impasse reached in mediation. When the parties submit a controversy to an arbitrator, they have agreed to be bound by the decision he/she renders. There is no appeal from an arbitrator's decision, and in most states it will be enforced by the courts.

Like other arbitration awards, an arbitrator's decision on spousal support and property division will be enforced in most states, although the courts are not as yet accustomed to doing so. In marital matters, courts hold to a doctrine known as *parens patriae* which is aimed at protecting "the best interests of the children" albeit with a rather poor record of success. Actually, the court seldom has either the time or the means to examine questions in any depth. Still, provisions for children in an arbitrator's decision, like an agreement of the parties, are subject to court sanction.

Arbitration is an adversarial process when the parties are represented by legal counsel. Lawyers are known as advocates—hence the term *adversarial process*. They must use every lawful means of asserting their clients' interests. The parties may also present their own cases to the arbitrator without an attorney. It is considerably easier to do this in an arbitration than in court. Even so, it is still an adversarial process because the parties, acting as advocates for themselves, compete with each other for a favorable decision by the arbitrator.

Arbitration offers the following advantages:

1. It is private. Only the parties, arbitrator, witnesses, and legal counsel (if any) may attend.
2. Hearings are scheduled to meet the convenience of the arbitrator, parties, witnesses, and legal counsel.
3. Hearings may be recessed when circumstances dictate, and continued at another agreed-upon time.
4. Hearings actually take place when scheduled.
5. Only the issues submitted will be considered by the arbitrator.
6. The hearing will take place within a matter of days or weeks after the issues are submitted.
7. The arbitrator has only *one* case to consider at a time.
8. The arbitrator is selected by the parties.
9. Outcomes are less dependent on the skill of legal counsel and upon technicalities.

The Marital Arbitration Rules provide guidelines and procedures similar to those of the Marital Mediation Rules. In practice, couples using the Marital Mediation Rules rarely resort to arbitration. Not one of the first hundred couples found it necessary to arbitrate an impasse. In several instances, the act of clearly stating the issue to be decided by the arbitrator resulted in their reaching agreement. Still, the inclusion of arbitration as part of the structured mediation process avoids the use of impasse as a bargaining strategy.

How It Works

When It Is Used

Mediation under the Marital Mediation Rules can be used in any of the following situations:

1. For negotiating a written settlement agreement when the parties intend only a legal separation and do not contemplate divorce
2. For negotiating a written settlement agreement which will be a binding civil contract and will also become part of a decree of divorce
3. For negotiating a revision of an existing divorce decree when there has been a change in financial conditions, the needs of the parties, or the children

Who Uses It

The divorcing population for which the present Marital Mediation Rules are designed may be generally described as follows:

Age range. Twenty-eight to forty-five with exceptions tending to fall beyond forty-five rather than under twenty-eight.

Duration of marriage. Six to fifteen years, with exceptions being longer than fifteen years.

Family income level. $18,000 to $30,000 annually, with exceptions exceeding $30,000.

Children. One to three.

Education. Two to four years of college, with a significant number of professionals having graduate degrees.

Property. Equity in a residence, two automobiles, and household furnishings.

Savings. Vary widely from an insignificant amount to a range of $5000 to $10,000 found in a variety of forms, such as savings accounts in banks, mutual funds, and real estate, in addition to the residence, miscellaneous stocks and bonds, and retirement plans. Investments in a business or profession can be considered savings, but these are difficult to evaluate.

Insurance. Hospitalization, medical, and life insurance on the life of the husband. The latter is either term insurance or ordinary life with policy loans outstanding.

Debt. Mortgage on residence and other real estate owned and credit cards from banks, oil companies, and department stores. Outstanding balances, other than real estate or business loans, are about $600.

A Common Limitation

Even though structured mediation is a vast improvement over the adversarial legal system, it cannot avoid a resolution which may require a reduction in life-style. This results from the need to support two households from an income that might have been barely sufficient to support one. The spouse who least wanted the divorce may find it difficult to accept this change and may feel cheated. The mediator can help this person understand these feelings and deal with them in a constructive way.

The Adversarial Legal System

How It Is Chosen

In places where mediation services are offered, divorcing couples can choose mediation as an alternative to the adversarial legal system. Choosing mediation is a deliberate act requiring the active participation of both parties. They must hear an explanation of the process, understand how it works, and sign a written contract agreeing to use it.

By contrast, choosing the adversarial legal system is considerably more subtle. The parties often do not realize they have made the choice until they find themselves caught up in it with apparently no way out. There is little or no explanation in advance of commitment. There is no offer of a choice between it and anything else.

Without their awareness, the choice is made for most couples when either one or both parties decide to consult an attorney. Often their purpose in seeking the consultation was to find an answer to the question, What are my legal rights? This would seem to be a rational beginning for dealing with a matter in which one is without prior experience. Most people do not have information in advance when they are confronted with death or divorce.

Lawyers, like undertakers, are presumed to have the answer to questions in their field, but unlike undertakers, lawyers never answer the questions. They are not answered because there *are* no answers to what the client wants to know.

There is no other field of law in which the court is given such complete and, for all practical purposes, uncontrolled discretion as in divorce cases. To answer the client's question, the lawyer would have to guess what the judge might do, except that one can never be sure which judge will hear the case. Studies have shown, and observers of the legal process confirm, that different judges may make quite different decisions upon substantially the same factual situation.

This uncertainty does not stop most lawyers from giving what sounds like an answer while qualifying each statement made. The one thing the client is very sure of from the consultation is that it is all very hard to understand. From this follows a decision to leave it up to the lawyer who then compliments the client for having made a very wise choice as a check for the retainer fee is written.

How It Works

Unfortunately the parties seldom visualize in advance how their situation could possibly turn into a bitter competitive struggle. Of course, they have heard of such things happening to others. They may have been agreed with each other that there has already been enough pain, so now "we will both go to the same lawyer and work out a fair settlement." Some may have worked out an agreement in advance on everything they believed was needed.

What they do not know about the adversarial system is that the lawyer, as an advocate, is required to represent, or advocate, *solely* the interest of his client. *He cannot represent both parties,* as is commonly supposed. The lawyer represents his client within the "light of his professional judgment." But the client's interest is always perceived as being in opposition to the interests of the other party. The lawyer cannot and does not regard the parties as having a common problem which he or she will help resolve.

The represented party, feeling that there is a knowledgeable person "on my side," experiences considerable relief after all the feelings of fear and helplessness that have gone before. At this point there is little awareness of being postured against the other party—"What should he/she have to fear from me?" The heightened feelings of fear and helplessness the *other* party experiences by not having anybody on his/her side are not anticipated.

It is rare that the employment of one attorney does not lead to the employment of a second, unless the parties simply do not have the financial resources. The need for a second attorney usually comes into focus when the parties realize that many areas of agreement are needed which they had not previously considered. The possible implications of an attorney's routine demands for financial disclosure can be so threatening as to send an unrepresented party to another attorney in a near panic.

Once a second attorney is employed, the only factor limiting escalation of the competitive struggle between husband and wife is the financial resources of the family. In some cases, the struggle may continue not just through the divorce, but for the lifetime of the parties.

Future Directions

An essential difference in approach between mediation and the adversarial legal system is that mediation fosters a cooperative orientation while the adversarial legal system places the parties in competitive opposition. Whatever may be said in support of the adversarial process for resolving other kinds of controversies, in marital disputes this competitive struggle is frequently more damaging for the marriage partners and their children than everything else that preceded it.

Beginnings of Change

Much of society and most members of the legal profession seem to stoically accept this destructive process. But the beginnings of change are being made through the establishment of conciliation courts in a few states. Even in these states, conciliation services are available only in urban areas. Besides, as unmandated services, they are vulnerable to every budget crisis.

Problems of Change

Changing from one system to another brings about dislocations for those who have an investment in the older system. The legal professionals now handling divorce matters would certainly be at an economic disadvantage in a different system in which substantial numbers of other professionals were employed.

Yet the legal profession can hardly claim a vested and exclusive right to handle marital disputes in a way which fosters bitterness and acrimony. More socially acceptable concerns will be expressed as a means of resisting change. For example, the profession's long opposition to no-fault divorce was asserted as a concern for family stability. Yet candid statements made in professional meetings revealed a less lofty concern—that reduced controversy in no-fault divorce cases would mean reduced income for lawyers. When the public clearly demanded no-fault divorce, lawyers lobbied to continue the fault system by adding the same old fault considerations to claims for spousal support and custody.

It must be added, however, that individual attorneys have most certainly been in the vanguard of progressive social change. The profession in general has been indifferent, and family law sections within it have been notably resistant to needed changes. During the last two years, mediation of marital disputes has received increasing recognition as a possible direction for change. Some courts have developed pilot programs, and a number of private services are beginning operations.

The social costs of following or not following any course of action are always difficult to measure. But even without objective evaluative studies, it seems apparent that resolving marital disputes through structured mediation is socially less costly than the present system. As a voluntary, client-supported alternative to the adversarial legal system, mediation provides both a helpful service for those who use it and a model that society may eventually adopt.

Suggested Readings

See Bibliography for complete references.

Wheeler, *No Fault Divorce.*
Bohannan, "The Six Stations of Divorce," *Divorce and After,* pp. 33-62.
Bohannan, "Divorce Chains," *Divorce and After,* pp. 283-300.
DeWolf, *Bonds of Acrimony.*
Kessler, *The American Way of Divorce.*

2 Aspects of Divorce Settlement

Dysfunctional Marriages

Staying Together

When one or both partners decide that their marriage is no longer viable, one of two choices can be made: remain together or leave each other. If they choose to remain together, the relationship may be characterized by silent misery and withdrawal, or by hostility and the imposition of physical or mental pain upon each other, with occasional excursions outside the marriage.

It is not the purpose of this work to examine the psychological reasons why marriage partners stay together under such conditions, but an often-stated reason is, "It's for the sake of the children." And yet divorce itself does not devastate children or inhibit their psychic development. It is the dysfunctional relationship between the marriage partners which may be damaging for them as well as the children. Both adults and children require tension-free environments in order to express their individuality and to gratify their emotional needs.

Leaving Each Other

Marriage partners may leave each other in one of three ways: death, abandonment, or divorce. Improved methods of health care have extended life expectancy—especially of women through safer childbirth—so that significantly fewer people are leaving the relationship by dying a natural death. On the other hand, most homicides (approximately 80 percent) take place within families or between persons who have a relationship to each other, and nearly all suicides are relationship-related. It follows, therefore, that a substantial number of marriages are ended by violent deaths.

Abandonment, though most often thought of as practiced by men, is a choice made by women as well. For example, during the Civil War, advertisements for runaway wives appeared side by side with those for runaway slaves. But abandonment has become a less effective choice than it once was with the poor and, occasionally, with the more affluent. People are more easily found through social security numbers, creditor's skip-trace services, and the recently developed computerized parent-locator system.

11

Divorce

Seen within the context of these other options, divorce clearly becomes the more rational and humane choice for the marriage partners and the children. Legal divorce does not signify that emotional divorce has preceded it or that it will follow at any particular time. Legal divorce simply gives sanction to the physical separation of the partners, thus putting an end to the ongoing bitterness and acrimony and opening up the possibility that one and perhaps both will eventually find a more fulfilling relationship.

Emotional divorce involves resolution and acceptance of the loss of the marital relationship with accompanying feelings toward self, spouse, family, friends, children, and work. It is a tragic fact that some former marriage partners spend the rest of their lives without resolving the issue of emotional divorce.

Increasingly in other countries, and more recently in the United States, we are coming to recognize that it is not rational to legally label one partner as responsible for the breakdown of a marital relationship. Legal fault findings and the procedures by which they are reached are as unconvincing and lacking in finality as the outcome of thirteenth-century debates over how many angels could stand on the head of a pin.

Settlement

What *does* matter is a fair settlement of affairs involving money and children which may be divided into the following interrelated categories:

Division of marital property

Spousal maintenance (alimony)

Child support

Custodial arrangements for children

Marital mediation is designed to deal solely with these settlement issues. But the objectives of settlement can be achieved only through the application of rational, cooperative processes. The mediator's skills and ingenuity are constantly challenged as he/she strives to keep settlement issues separated from emotional issues which could frustrate the mediation process.

One of the more significant reasons why the adversarial legal system has not achieved more satisfactory results has been the mixing of emotionally charged cause-of-divorce issues with settlement issues. Recently some enlightened courts and legislatures have allowed the separation of these issues by permitting the divorce to be granted while reserving the settlement issues for later determination.

A cooperative resolution of settlement issues often results in a resolution of emotional issues. In some instances, couples have been able to resume a satisfactory marital relationship following resolution of settlement issues in mediation.

Marital Mediation Rules

The four settlement categories mentioned above and in the Marital Mediation Rules have been derived from an examination of the laws of states that have comprehensively revised their divorce laws within the last five years. These states have followed the provisions of the Uniform Marriage and Divorce Act developed by the Commissioners on Uniform State Laws and have made improvements upon it in some areas. Because it is possible for the Family Mediation Association (FMA) to revise its Marital Mediation Rules to reflect the results of its own research and that of others, the marital mediation process can stay several years ahead of even the most responsive and enlightened state legislatures and many years ahead of the less responsive ones.

On the other hand, state laws will rarely, if ever, exclude voluntary use of the rules. Where use of the rules is limited by state law, it is likely to affect the mediation process only in minor respects and certainly would not preclude its use. Thus in most or perhaps all states, the rules may be successfully adopted and used by divorcing couples.

Marital Property

Even though the language of the rules is intended to be precise and must prevail over any simplified explanation, it still seems worthwhile to offer one at this point. Under the mediation rules, marital property is defined by exclusion. This means that all property owned by either spouse, individually or jointly, is marital property unless it can be shown that the property is excluded for one of the following reasons:

1. The property was acquired by gift or inheritance or is property which was exchanged for such property.
2. The property was acquired prior to the marriage or is property which was exchanged for such property.

3. The property was acquired by either spouse after legal separation or divorce.
4. The property was excluded by agreement of the parties.
5. The increase in value of nonmarital property has resulted from so-called passive ownership.
6. When increases in value of nonmarital property have resulted from both active and passive ownership, an allocation must be made so as to exclude increases attributable to passive ownership.

Under the rules, *active ownership* is inferred from the owner's having made capital improvements and other efforts intended to enhance the value of the property during the marital relationship. *Passive ownership* means that the owner did nothing to enhance the value of the property, so that any increase in its value would result solely from market and other economic conditions.

In most instances, there will be little or no difficulty in identifying which property is marital property, and thus subject to division. In some cases, however, where the marriage has been of long duration and property holdings, gifts, or inheritances are substantial, the identification of marital property can become an extremely complex problem.

Determining Its Value. Once marital property has been identified, the first step toward making a division is to establish values. Frequently the parties can agree on the value of the property. If the property is to be sold and the proceeds are to be divided by agreement of the parties, there is no problem.

But when agreement cannot be reached, the mediator may arrange for an impartial appraisal to be made. Complex problems of valuation may involve such things as the worth of a business, vested retirement plans, and beneficial interests under trusts. In most instances, advice on how to go about resolving such problems will be needed from an accountant, actuary, or attorney.

Types of Divisions. Once the identity and value of marital property are established, the next problem is to consider the character and form of the property. This is important since a division of property can be accomplished in three ways:
1. *Division in kind.* This means that the property is divided in such a way that each person becomes sole and exclusive owner of a share. This is easily accomplished, for example, with such things as stocks and bonds which can be divided into separate certificates without the necessity of sale.
2. *Joint ownership.* This is very simple and easy to accomplish, but may raise questions about how the property will be maintained and managed. Certain properties, such as a going business, may be so sensitive to management that divided ownership and operational responsibility could quickly cause the business to fail.

3. *Sale of property* with agreed-upon division of net proceeds. The parties must first agree to the sale price. Then they must agree to what costs of sale shall be deductible in arriving at a net sales price which will be divided between them.

Who Gets How Much? Next the parties must decide what proportionate share of marital property each is to receive. While some states call for an arbitrary 50 percent division of marital property and some couples decide to divide it this way, the rules do not call for any particular percentage division.

A useful rationale is to begin with a 50-50 division of marital property between the marriage partners. Then they can consider circumstances which would justify revising that division. A consideration of the following factors may suggest such a change:

1. *The contribution of each spouse* to the acquisition of marital property. The contribution of a spouse as a homemaker may be sufficient to support an equal division of marital property. But if that spouse has also worked outside the home and contributed her earnings, this may suggest a division in her favor. On the other hand, if the wife personally performed few homemaking services and did not work outside the home, this might suggest a division in favor of the husband.
2. *The economic circumstances* of each party should be considered. The property owned as capital assets by the supporting spouse and the resulting credit available to that spouse may significantly influence his/her ability to produce investment income. When a large part of the income is of this type, it may suggest an unequal division of property in his/her favor and result in an increase in the payment of support to the dependent spouse.

    Another economic circumstance is the fact that certain properties require management expertise or high mortgage payments. They must be either sold or awarded to the supporting spouse who has the expertise and the higher income needed to meet the payments. In some cases the parties may also agree that market conditions are such that it would be impractical or unwise to sell and divide the proceeds.
3. *Housing needs* of the custodial parent may be such that they would dictate an allocation of the residence to that party, with the result that there is an unequal division of property.
4. *The ownership of separate property* by either spouse may influence whether an equal or unequal division is indicated. For example, when there is great disparity between the individual wealth of the parties, the allocation of an insignificant 50 percent of marital property to an already wealthy spouse may lack a reasonable rationale.

5. *A dependent spouse may prefer* a high level of support to an equal distribution of property in some cases.

Spousal Support

The terms *spousal maintenance* or *spousal support* are used interchangeably with the traditional term *alimony*. These new terms are used in no-fault divorce laws (which also change *divorce* to *dissolution*) to signify that a different approach is taken when couples decide to terminate their marriages.

The no-fault approach allows the court to find that the marriage is no longer working in such a way that there can be societal or personal advantage to family members in continuing its legal existence. In legal terms this means the marriage is *irretrievably broken* and that there are *irreconcilable differences*.

Who Is the Dependent Spouse? As to the needs of the dependent spouse—today almost invariably the wife—the no-fault approach supports the position of social scientists and growing numbers of men and women that the wife shall be treated as an equal partner with her husband. For this reason, in no-fault legislation and the Marital Mediation Rules, the dependent spouse may be either the husband or the wife. Common Law provided alimony for the wife, except under certain circumstances related to fault, but never for the husband in any case.[1]

The life-style of the parties and the economic realities of the marriage partnership dictate which marriage partner can be identified as the dependent spouse. Dependency of one spouse upon the other is influenced by which spouse has been largely responsible for the uncompensated job of providing for the daily needs of the children, the home, and the family social life.

Differences in earning ability may have developed because of the agreed-upon need for one parent to be at home instead of working outside the home in ways that would have maintained marketable skills. One must recognize, too, that some men still insist that their wives stay home even though there may be little or no reason why they should do so. A wife's contribution to the family through work outside the home may be perceived by these men as a failure on their part to fulfill their provider role.

In general, it can be said that the concept of spousal maintenance is aimed at achieving *the highest degree of financial independence of the former husband and wife at the earliest possible time.* Despite legal provisions for lifetime alimony, few women actually need it and few men can afford it. The concept of spousal maintenance conforms more closely to the actual behavior most often followed by formerly married persons. One has to search hard to find examples of women who have been able to enjoy a long life of leisure through support payments provided by a former husband. In such rare cases, the former husband is most likely a man of considerable affluence, a man consumed by guilt, or a combination of both.

How Much is Enough? In arriving at the proper amount of spousal maintenance, the basic considerations are

1. *The needs of the dependent spouse* and the ability of the supporting spouse to meet such needs while meeting his own and that of others who are dependent upon him. The dependent spouse may have a substantial employment disability as a result of not having been employed outside the home for many years. This may be partially or wholly remedied by payment of rehabilitative support for a limited time to enable her to achieve new skills, update earlier training, and maximize her ability to become self-supporting.
2. *The character and amount of marital property* apportioned to her. At times, marital property may not be easy to divide. Thus a larger level of spousal maintenance will be needed to offset the disproportionate division of property.
3. *The standard of living* established during the marriage. But both parties should realize that establishing two households in place of one may call for a reduction in their life-style.
4. *The possible vesting of the wife's social security benefits* as a result of her marriage. At present, her benefits become vested after twenty years of marriage. Proposals have been introduced in Congress which would reduce the time for vesting to ten years. (Coincidentally, many marriages seem to go through periods of crisis at around the point of ten and twenty years' duration.) Thus, if the couple is in mediation at a time which is six months to a year away from vesting of social security rights in the wife, it is wise to defer legal divorce until vesting has occurred rather than have the wife forfeit these benefits.
5. *Tax advantages* may result from the payment of spousal maintenance. These will be discussed in a later chapter. For example, child support may be partially or completely combined with spousal maintenance so that the entire payment can be treated, for tax purposes, as spousal maintenance.
6. *The duration of the marriage* and the age and physical and emotional condition of the spouse seeking maintenance, as well as the one called upon to provide it, all require consideration.

Child Support

Sharing Responsibility. In the past, most states have put the full responsibility for child support upon the father. However, as of this writing, all but eleven states have made this a shared responsibility of both the father and the mother. Here again the law has tended to follow the behavioral patterns of society. The male's image as provider has been considerably blemished by the developing evidence that women have been and are providing substantially the support of their children.

On the other hand, during the last hundred years, women have consistently sought, and in nearly all instances been awarded, custody of children. The fault implications which have been associated with divorce have often cast the father in the role of the bad or rejected parent—a role which has reduced his incentive to meet support obligations. If the situation had been reversed and custody had been awarded to fathers rather than mothers—with mothers receiving the blame—it is doubtful mothers would have established a higher record of fulfilling support obligations than fathers.

The current trend toward shared support responsibility, as well as shared parenting, offers the hope that both parents will be able to cooperate to provide a better and more supportive environment for the development of their children, even though they lead separate lives.

Deciding How Much. Among the factors which should be considered in determining child support are the following:

1. *The financial resources of the child.* For example, the child may have received an inheritance from a grandparent, uncle, or aunt which may provide substantially toward his/her support.
2. *The financial resources of the custodial parent.* It is likely that both parents will have to use not only their income but other resources to provide support for their minor children.
3. *The financial resources and needs of the other parent.* Obviously, both parents must be able to meet their reasonable financial and emotional needs if they are to provide financial and other support for their children.
4. *The standard of living* established by the family prior to the dissolution of the marriage. Both parties must decide whether the maintenance of two households rather than one may call for a reduction in life-style.
5. *The physical and emotional condition of the child*, as well as his or her educational needs. Certain children have unusual physical or emotional disabilities which call for medical or psychological treatment and perhaps special education.

Child Custody

In the adversarial legal system, controversies over custody are common and are frequently used by parents as a tactic to gain financial leverage. But in marital mediation, controversies over custody are rare with the major contentions centering on visitation arrangements for the noncustodial parent. This experience tends to support what matrimonial lawyers have been saying—that most custody fights are really financial squabbles.

Under the Marital Mediation Rules, if there *is* a controversy regarding custody, all financial matters must first be resolved in the form of a legally binding contractual settlement before the issues of custody will be considered. Thus the children are not allowed to be used as financial pawns in what is ostensibly a concern for their proper custody.

Guidelines for Determining Custody. Regardless of what guidelines are used, there is frequently no rational basis for determining that one parent rather than the other shall be the custodial parent. This dilemma is well stated by Judge Susanne Sedgwick of the Hennepin County Family Court, Minneapolis, Minnesota:

There are two areas in which decisions are difficult to make—because there is no basis for decision. One is when both parents are equally excellent parents as far as their respective abilities to give the proper care, love, affection, and attention to the child, and who have an equally good relationship with the child at the time they come into court. When both parents are absolutely equal, there is really very little basis for a decision. The other area is when both parents are equally deficient in parenting skills. Again, there is very little basis for decision.

Usually the court decides which parent should have custody based on a number of factors. I think I'll just list the guidelines set down by the [Minnesota] legislature to be considered by the court.

1. The love, affection and other emotional ties existing between the competing parties and the child or children.
2. The capacity and disposition of the competing parties to give the child love, affection, attention, or guidance and continuation of the education and the raising of the child in its religion or creed, if any.
3. The capacity and disposition of competing parties to provide the child with food, clothing, medical care, etc.
4. The length of time that the child has lived in a stable satisfactory environment and the desirability of maintaining continuity. (This item becomes more important the younger the child is. Short periods of time from an adult perspective may seem like an eternity to a very young child.)
5. The cultural background of the child.
6. The permanence as a family unit of the existing or proposed custodial home.
7. The home, school, and community record of the child.
8. The reasonable preference of the child, if the court deems the youngster is old enough to give a preference.
9. Any other factor considered by the court to be relevant.

The legislature has also directed that the court is not to prefer one parent over the other on the basis of sex alone.[2]

Responsibilities of Parents. In mediation of custody under the Marital Mediation Rules, Sections 34 and 35 of the rules provide specific parenting responsibilities for both parents. Thus visitation is not merely a privilege or right of the noncustodial parent, but an important and significant part of the total parenting which will be provided for the children.

The rules provide that the custodial parent may determine issues relating to the child's upbringing—including education, health care, and religious training—even over the objections of the noncustodial parent. In a forthcoming book entitled *The Disposable Parent,* Dr. Melvin Roman suggests that these areas may also be effectively managed as a part of shared parenting under a joint-custody arrangement.[3] (Dr. Roman is a professor in the Department of Psychiatry, Albert Einstein College of Medicine, in New York.) The rationale of rules 34 and 35 is based on the widely held belief that a single parent needs the authority of a custodial parent in order to facilitate decision making and avoid impasses.

Joint Custody. An option provided under Section 36 of the rules, joint custody is a controversial concept. In many cases, state laws neither provide for it nor specifically prohibit it. Courts will rarely order it against the wishes of the parties, and some judges may refuse to sanction it even when the parties wish to have this arrangement. But Dr. Roman found that couples who place themselves in a joint and equal authority relationship tend to cooperate with one another.

This contrasts with the relationship created by designating one parent as the custodial parent and giving that parent final authority to make decisions. Regardless of what may be said about making cooperative decisions, it has been demonstrated time and again that designating one parent as the ultimate authority figure over the children in divorce proceedings has set the stage for years of controversy.

When parents agree upon a joint-custody arrangement, a lawful civil contract has been established even if the court will not enforce it and if, against their wishes, it designates one of them as custodial parent. The parties may still decide to follow their agreement rather than the arrangement the court has imposed upon them. In practice, many parents have been doing exactly this all along with apparently good results.

What arrangement is in the best interests of the children? We agree with those authorities who say that the *relationship between the parents* is by far the most significant factor, although we are not unmindful of the importance of the child's peer relationships in a neighborhood or school and of his/her need for a certain stability in life, life-style, and living arrangements. All these and other relevant factors should be taken into account in working out living arrangements even when there is joint custody. Joint custody does not mean that the children will live equal lengths of time with each parent or that there will be constant movement back and forth between them.

Involving the Children. It will come as no surprise to family therapists that marriage partners confronting divorce do not know as much as they think they know about what their children want. It is possible that the children may have been attempting to find a way of bringing the parents back together by manipulating custody or visiting arrangements. Other children may feel responsible for their parents' troubles and may go to extremes in an attempt to please both parents impartially or to avoid having either parent feel rejected by them.

With these thoughts in mind, parents should be encouraged to bring the children to all mediation sessions regarding custody and visitation, if they are old enough to comprehend what is happening. In beginning to work with parents and children, the mediator should see to it that the children understand that a decision must be made and should explain to them exactly what decisions are needed. It should be made clear that both parents will still be parents and neither will be rejected by whatever decision is made. It should also be explained that the decision does *not* mean making a choice of one parent over the other, but deciding how the family will function when the parents are living separately. It will be helpful if the parents reinforce what the mediator has said by restating the same things in their own way.

It is important that a tone of openness and frankness be established from the very beginning, so that each parent and child have full opportunity to say exactly what he or she thinks or feels. Usually the children are already living with one parent. If the mediator suspects that children may have been told what to say and what not to say in the mediation session, the mediator may begin by asking the children, "What were you told not to say in here?" This can set the stage for openness and establish the rule that there are to be no secrets.

Managing Controversy. When there is an issue between the parents about custody, it is almost always wise for the mediator to establish agreement on visitation arrangements for the noncustodial parent before a decision is made about which parent will be the noncustodial one. The mediator may also use the custody sessions to help the family work out problems which will surely arise later on as they begin to work with the arrangement they have agreed upon.

It is also well to remember that no custodial arrangement is ever permanent. The parties may agree upon a particular arrangement for a period of time with the stipulation that it will be specifically reviewed at the end of the period. Court orders are naturally required to bring about a legal change whether it is agreed upon by the parties or is otherwise decided by the court.

Even though property, spousal maintenance, child support, and custody are interrelated, the rules give the mediator the power to determine when a particular issue is settled and to prohibit the parties from reopening the issue without good cause. Experience has shown that without management by the mediator, parties may conditionally close issues with the intention of opening them later. If parties are allowed the unhampered privilege of reopening previously settled issues, it will quickly become a leverage tactic. But the mediator should exercise discretion and allow the reopening of previously settled issues in the interest of facilitating the settlement of subsequent issues.

Suggested Readings

See Bibliography for complete references.

Orientation, Part I, Appendix FMA-A.
Orientation, Part II, Appendix FMA-B.
Marital Mediation Rules, Appendix FMA-C.
Bass and Rein, *Divorce or Marriage.*
Gettleman and Markowitz, *The Courage to Divorce.*
Epstein, *Divorced in America.*
Women in Transition, Inc., *Women in Transition.*

Footnotes

1. As this goes to the press, the U.S. Supreme Court has just agreed to consider a case that would decide whether the laws of the thirteen states that make no provision for the husband to receive alimony are constitutional.

2. Speech delivered to annual meeting of the Association of Family Conciliation Courts, Minneapolis, Minn., May 1977.

3. Melvin Roman, "The Disposable Parent," *Conciliation Courts Review* 15, 2 (December 1977):1.

3 How Structured Mediation Works

The Need for Structure

Asking a couple to engage in rational, cooperative negotiation and decision making over apportionment of the tangible evidence of their shattered dreams may seem to be asking the impossible. The very thought of undertaking the task is viewed by some as so overwhelming that they feel utterly helpless.

Whatever attorneys may say in their initial consultation, most clients have already decided to place the entire matter in an attorney's hands. Clients feel welcome relief at the close of the first interview after they have paid the retainer fee. What clients do by contacting an attorney is to place their problem in what they perceive as a structured system requiring little active participation on their part. It is only later that they gradually come to realize that the lawyer cannot and will not handle everything. There is still a substantial measure of work and responsibility which clients must assume if lawyers are to fulfill their role as advocates in an effective manner.

In the course of marital dissolution, conflicts call for rational, not emotional, problem-solving techniques. The matters at stake are reality issues associated with underlying feelings that interfere with resolution. Since the decisions made will have an impact of such long duration, the adoption of a facilitative structure within which settlement can be reached is essential.

The structure provided by attorneys and the adversarial legal system invites many clients to avoid personal responsibility and to look for easy solutions. In mediation, the client is less able to engage in such fantasies and avoid responsibility. When a couple agrees to reach settlement through mediation under the Marital Mediation Rules, a clear, detailed structure and frame of reference are chosen which call for their active participation and assumption of personal responsibility.

Legal Structure

It seems axiomatic that the higher the level of stress, the greater is the need for a clear, unambiguous structure. The adversarial legal system is lauded as a highly structured, rational system. It is understandable, then, that many laymen imagine that marital matters are handled by the courts in a clear and rationally structured manner. But most divorcing couples experience a stunning disillusionment—a disillusionment that is now being validated by research findings. An in-depth, six-year study showed that those couples who were not able to reach their own settlements and sought recourse in the courts came back again and again with further settlement controversies.[1]

The divorce laws of most states detail the rights and responsibilities of the parties in only the most general way. In addition, the judge in divorce matters is given much broader discretion by far than in any other field of law, including criminal law where the judge's discretion is broad indeed.

In a study of the reasons given for deciding custody in appellate court decisions compared to legislative guidelines, it has been found that most courts seem to pay little attention to the guidelines. Instead, recourse is made to other court decisions or to simplistic, unsupported reasoning as exemplified by the "tender-years doctrine."[2] This doctrine asserts that the mother is the only proper custodian for children of so-called tender years. In each case, judges decide whether the children qualify for this vague age category.

When a judge has exercised discretion, there is little the parties can do about it. The appellate courts will not disturb the lower-court judge's decision, except in instances in which it has been obviously and callously abused. Many judges themselves experience stress in attempting to exercise wisely the discretion given them. It is commonly exercised in the absence of needed factual information as well as sufficient time for consideration.

Difficult as it often is for them to talk to each other, it is a wise decision when couples choose to work out their own settlement instead of abdicating that power to others. Even though divorcing couples often feel helpless and confused, all but the more severely dysfunctional can negotiate a settlement if a structure is provided within which to do so. The parties obviously have more information and feeling for their life situation than any lawyer, judge, jury, or arbitrator can possibly gain in the course of the brief contacts provided by legal hearings.

Structure of the Rules

Mediation Center

The specific structure of marital mediation is best defined by the rules, but a general understanding can be gained from a discussion of the various roles created by the rules. The Family Mediation Association or an authorized mediation center serves as the administrator in mediation and arbitration proceedings. FMA also performs other work in research, development, and training of marital mediators and arbitrators; supervision of mediation centers; and presentation of educational programs for the general public.

As administrator, a center provides the following:

1. *Physical facilities* in which mediation may be conducted. The feeling that one is on neutral yet friendly and supportive territory contributes significantly toward fostering the trust and cooperative attitudes needed in marital mediation.
2. *Orientation* provided by staff persons so that those considering mediation may have a full and complete explanation of rules and procedures.
3. *A neutral communications center* through which the parties may communicate with one another, the mediator, and the advisory attorney, while observing the rule not to communicate with either the mediator or the advisory attorney outside the presence of each other.
4. *A panel of trained mediators* from which a mediator is selected whose training and experience appear best suited to meet the needs of each couple. Specific training, experience, and supervision are required of all FMA-certified marital mediators as a condition for membership on the panel. Upgrading of their training will be required by FMA from time to time to maintain panel membership.
5. *A panel of impartial advisory attorneys.* Attorneys who are not on the panel may be selected by the parties provided they agree to abide by the rules relating to impartial advisory attorneys. Any attorney may make application for membership on the panel. If it appears from an examination of the attorney's background and experience that he or she is adequately trained and enjoys a respectable professional reputation, membership on the panel is available upon completion of an FMA-approved orientation program.

   FMA requires that its panel attorneys have a high degree of skill in drafting settlement agreements, as well as knowledge of domestic-relations law and tax implications of marital dissolution. An insight into the complexity of the problems confronting the advisory attorney in drafting a settlement agreement may be gained by examining the Guide for Negotiating and Drafting Marital Settlement Agreements (Appendix FMA-E).
6. *Escrow deposit and accounting service* is provided by the center. At the beginning of mediation, a deposit is made by the clients. As mediation proceeds, charges are made against this deposit for mediation fees, advisory attorney fees, or any other resource person or persons called upon by the parties and the mediator.

   Charges by mediators and attorneys are made on an hourly basis at a rate established by agreement with the parties. Charges by resource persons are subject to negotiation in each case. When mediation is completed, the center makes an accounting for all funds received and disburses payment according to charges incurred. Any unused portion of the deposit is refunded to the client.

7. *Files* of all active cases in mediation. Files are transferred into record storage as mediations are completed.
8. *Interpretation of the Marital Mediation Rules* and resolution of controversies between the parties and the mediator about application of the rules.
9. *Appointment of a mediator or impartial advisory attorney* in the event of a vacancy due to disability, death, resignation, or if for any other reason the mediator or advisory attorney fails to serve.
10. *Evaluation* of the work done by marital mediators and advisory attorneys.

Mediator

Mediators must be impartial and unbiased, yet must see to it that both parties observe the rules. In doing this, they may easily be seen by one party as actively supporting the other. For example, if either party is failing to make full and complete financial disclosure, it is the mediator's duty to see to it that this person provides the information, even though the party called upon may feel the mediator has become an advocate for the other.

Maintaining Control. The most important function of the mediator is to maintain clear, firm control over the manner in which negotiations are conducted. Of course, the best control is that which is least noticeable. Perhaps one of the more effective means of control at the disposal of the mediator is the power to open and close negotiation of various issues. If negotiations in a particular area appear to be counterproductive, the mediator can temporarily close that issue and move on to another which, if resolved, may contribute to successful resolution of the more difficult issue.

Approving the Agreement. While clients must be permitted the greatest autonomy in reaching settlement, mediators must eventually confront their responsibility for either concurring or not concurring in the settlement reached by the couple. This calls for a high degree of sensitivity and thoughtful consideration on the part of mediators. Even though their nonconcurrence does not invalidate any agreement reached by the parties, it can have a significant impact on whether the court will approve the settlement.

The mediator's nonconcurrence is a means by which the mediation center may disassociate itself from a clearly unfair settlement agreement and protect its reputation for fairness. Even though the mediator's nonconcurrence has no legal impact, psychologically it is a most powerful form of intervention. In practice, it will be used only when an agreement is reached which is manifestly not in keeping with the ethical and legal responsibilities of the parties—if, for example, a mother agrees to assume full responsibility for the support of the children despite the father's ability to contribute to their support.

Evaluating the Settlement. The possibility that a party may call for an evaluation of the settlement reached under section 40 of the rules may have a beneficial influence on the way the parties negotiate. Thus a party might be less motivated to negotiate a skewed agreement if the opposite party is likely to reject it after evaluation.

The responsibility of mediators to provide an evaluation may motivate them to be more thorough in seeing to it that all needed provisions are included in the agreement. It will be embarrassing to the mediator if omissions in the agreement are pointed out—items which the parties would have included had the mediator suggested them during mediation.

On the other hand, mediators must be cautious not to allow the parties to draw them into an ongoing evaluative process during mediation. This could lead to the agreement becoming more that of the mediators than of the parties. Such a result would defeat the most fundamental of all principles of mediation—that the agreement be one for which *each party takes full responsibility.*

The mediator needs to understand the Guide for Negotiating and Drafting Marital Settlement Agreements found in Appendix FMA-E. The advisory attorney has the legal training required to apply this guide in drafting settlement agreements, but both the mediator and the attorney can use it as a general check list for possible provisions.

Advisory Attorney

While the role of impartial advisory attorney is a newly created role for lawyers, they have demonstrated the ability to move from the role of advocate into impartial roles, such as judge or arbitrator. They make these transitions quite easily and often serve with distinction in the impartial role. Thus the role of impartial advisory attorney in marital mediations is well within the range of the lawyer's capabilities even though it will be viewed with skepticism by some.

The Settlement Document. The advisory attorney first appears when the mediator and the couple believe they have arrived at a workable settlement arrangement. It is this tentative agreement, explained by the parties and the mediator, that the attorney must refine into a clearly worded settlement agreement in a relatively short time. The agreement must be one that can be understood and followed by the parties in their ongoing relationship after divorce.

The attorney's knowledge, experience, and sensitivity in addressing the needs of the family's postdivorce relationships (including support, custody, and visitation) must equal his/her professional skill in dealing with property, legal questions, and tax-saving options. The lawyer's impartiality must be beyond question. When he/she has a full grasp of the settlement arrangements developed by the mediator and the parties, then the attorney must draft the settlement document. Later, he/she presents the document to the parties, making sure that it is in conformity with their agreement.

Adding Provisions. Normally, attorneys add a significant number of provisions, called "boilerplate," which were never considered by either the mediator or the parties, but which are designed to facilitate the postdivorce relationship between the parties and reinforce the specific agreements actually reached. These provisions affect the form rather than the substance of the agreement reached by the parties. They will be explained to the parties by the attorney when the document is presented.

An example is the provision that the written agreement is the entire contract, thus ruling out the possibility that a party may later claim that the written agreement was made in consideration of an oral agreement. Another example is a warranty or representation on the part of each party regarding the accuracy of his or her disclosures about property and earnings. There are other similar provisions which, depending upon the nature of the settlement, the skillful attorney will include in the agreement without the request of either party.

Process

The process called for in the rules is designed to make the mediation procedure orderly. For example, the rules require that mediation sessions be conducted on a weekly basis. If the parties fail to proceed with mediation after ten days' notice, their deposit will be forfeited. There are also instructions to the parties about how to proceed in certain situations, such as predivorce settlements, separation agreements, postdivorce modifications, arbitration of an impasse, and court enforcement of temporary settlement agreements. The issue guidelines for property division, support, and custody discussed in chapter 2 provide a rational frame of reference or structure within which settlement is reached.

An understanding of the process can best be gained from a careful reading and understanding of the Marital Mediation Rules found in Appendix FMA-C. Understanding how to apply the rules is essential for the successful conduct of marital mediation. "Orientation, Part II" in the Appendix will also be helpful.

Suggested Readings

See Bibliography for complete references.

Orientation, Part I, Appendix FMA-A.
Orientation, Part II, Appendix FMA-B.
Marital Mediation Rules, Appendix FMA-C.
Janis and Mann, *Decision Making.*
Rheinstein, *Marriage Stability, Divorce, and the Law.*

Notes

1. This study was conducted by Robert J. Levy, professor of law, and Julie A. Fulton, law research fellow and Ph.D. candidate in sociology, University of Minnesota Law School. It is now in the final stages of completion. Preliminary findings were reported by Julie A. Fulton at the annual meeting of the Association of Family and Conciliation Courts, Minneapolis, Minn., May 16, 1977.

2. An unpublished study conducted by O.J. Coogler, J.D., and Nancy Foster, J.D. candidate, Emory University Law School.

4 The Marital Mediation Procedure

Orientation

The first step in the mediation process is to provide information to clients. When they contact the center, pamphlets may be mailed out free of charge. If further interest is expressed in mediation, the couple should be asked to make an appointment for an intake interview.

Two identical packages containing materials found in the appendixes will be furnished to each party at intake with a cover letter suggesting that the parties read them in this sequence:

1. Orientation, Part I (FMA-A)
2. Orientation, Part II (FMA-B)
3. Marital Mediation Rules (FMA-C)
4. Forms for Use in Marital Mediation (FMA-G)
   a. Personal Data and Information (FMA 177)
   b. Financial and Income Statement (FMA 277)
   c. Monthly Expense Budget (FMA 377)
   d. Emergencies and Future Goals (FMA 377A)
   e. Seasonal Expenses (FMA 377B)
   f. Installment Debt Payments (FMA 377C)
5. Analysis of Family Expenditures (FMA 477)
6. Predivorce Mediation-Arbitration Agreement (FMA 577)
   or
   Postdivorce Mediation-Arbitration Agreement (FMA 677)
7. Temporary Custody and Maintenance Agreement (FMA 777)
8. Audiotape Release (FMA 1377)

Couples should be encouraged to come to the office to receive this material at an intake interview rather than having it mailed to them. A charge may be made for this interview and the materials furnished.

A second appointment may be made with a staff person after enough time has passed for husband and wife to read the furnished material. The procedure to be followed during this meeting with the staff person is to verify that the parties have read "Orientation," parts I and II, and the mediation rules. Questions are answered. Then the couple signs the mediation agreement (FMA 577 or 677) and makes the fee deposit. This must cover ten hours of mediation and services of the advisory attorney.

31

A determination must be made during this appointment of whether there is controversy over custody. If it appears that there is, then the couple must furnish an additional budget so that all budget information will be completed in advance of the first mediation session.

First Two-Hour Session

Mediation sessions are usually scheduled for two hours. It is desirable that the mediator spend the first few minutes getting acquainted with husband and wife, putting them at ease as much as possible and suggesting a general procedure which may be followed for working toward a settlement. It is important that they feel they are genuinely participating in the development of an agenda for settlement, rather than having one imposed upon them.

It is likely that the parties can reach agreement about procedural matters. This will provide the mediator the first opportunity to compliment them for their willingness to cooperate with each other. Particularly at this stage, the mediator must be alert to opportunities for positively reinforcing each instance of cooperative behavior.

The Agenda

While the mediator is free to work out any agenda he and the couple can agree upon, the following agenda has been found to be workable:

1. Temporary support and custody arrangements
2. Identification of and division of marital property
3. Spousal maintenance
4. Child support
5. Child custody and visitation arrangements

In the event the couple has not reached agreement on which of them will be the custodial parent, certain contingency agreements may have to be reached about property allocations. For example, the couple may agree that the custodial parent will have the use of the family residence until the children reach an agreed-upon age. It is sufficient to explain that such contingencies can be included, while avoiding detailed discussion of these issues during adoption of an agenda.

Financial Forms

Having brought about agreement on an agenda, the mediator next looks over the budget, financial statement, and income forms presented by the couple. If the parties need to do further work on their budgets or provide other information, the mediator should point this out to them and obtain their agreement to have it completed by the next session. If a party is experiencing difficulty in obtaining information needed to complete the budget, these problems may be explored and suggestions made by the mediator.

No opportunity should be overlooked for getting the couple to perform simple cooperative tasks, such as furnishing bank statements or check stubs. If the mediator believes the husband and wife can help each other develop their budgets, this too can be highly useful. For example, the wife may be very helpful to the husband in estimating his food, laundry, and general household budget. The husband, on the other hand, may be very helpful to the wife in estimating the cost of an automobile, insurance, repairs, and the like.

The mediator should be careful not to assign tasks in sensitive areas which are likely to lead to arguments. In some instances, it may even be necessary for one party or the other to get a third person to help. When this is done, it is important that this person be named in advance and agreed upon by both parties. If the opposite party is uncomfortable with the choice, another source of help may be offered.

Temporary Settlement Agreement

The objective of the temporary settlement agreement (Appendix FMA-G, Form FMA 777), is to stabilize the relationship between the parties during the time they are in mediation. They will then be able to work toward a permanent settlement with a minimum of controversy over financial and other arrangements. Only the standard items which need to be agreed upon are indicated by blanks in the temporary agreement. These are such matters as child support, spousal maintenance, mortgage or rent payments on the house or apartment, custody and visitation, joint assets, and joint charge accounts.

In helping the couple work out the support items of the temporary agreement, they should be reassured that any agreement reached does not set a precedent for the permanent agreement. *The purpose of the temporary agreement is simply to maintain the status quo during mediation.* Even though the couple will have already worked on their budgets, detailed consideration of items is not needed in reaching a temporary agreement. But it is important that the dependent spouse know what support will be provided and the supporting spouse know what payments he or she will be expected to make.

In most instances, the temporary agreement will have a duration of less than two months. Consequently, even if the parties make a substantial error in arriving at the amount of support, no lasting damage is likely to result. Detailed discussions of the budget must be avoided and the couple encouraged to reach agreement more or less on an intuitive basis. An estimate of their monthly expenditures is sufficient.

Special Stipulations. Other items which require attention must be included under special stipulations. The mediator should determine the outstanding balance on all bank charge cards and other charge accounts. Agreement must be reached on who will be responsible for the present balances, and this fact must be entered as part of the special stipulations.

A stipulation should also be included indicating which party will use each account and will be solely responsible for future charges to that account. If both parties wish to continue using the same bank credit card, then one party should establish a new and separate account and make no further charges on the old account.

In the event there are joint holdings such as checking accounts, savings accounts, stocks, bonds, and the like, they must be listed in paragraph 11 of FMA 777 under which the parties agree that there shall be no withdrawals or any other change in ownership for the duration of the contract. If there are to be any exceptions to this provision, they must be specified under "additional stipulations."

Other Sensitive Issues. If one party wants to remove personal items from the residence, agreement must be reached on what items will be removed (preferably by making a list) and when the move will take place. If this is not known, the parties must agree on how much notice must be given before the items agreed upon can be moved. Occasionally there may be other sensitive issues requiring agreement, such as ownership of pets, a photographic darkroom, a pottery kiln, a boat, a camper, house plants, and so on.

When the couple has reached agreement on the temporary contract and signed it within the first mediation hour, as most couples do, here is another opportunity for the mediator to compliment them on their cooperation. The temporary agreement is indeed a significant accomplishment. It represents an approximation of the final, permanent agreement which is the objective of the mediation process. Both a useful instrument and shaping behavior have been produced.

Second Hour

If there is no controversy over custody, the parties should now agree upon visitation arrangements. Provided the parties are willing, the mediator may schedule an additional special session for working out these arrangements at which the children will be present. This is a highly recommended procedure, but it may require an additional deposit because it is not included in the initial ten-hour deposit.

Marital Property

Now the mediator may turn to a consideration of marital property. Generally this will be fairly simple. It may consist, let us say, of an equity in a home, household furnishings, and one or two automobiles. This can be determined from an examination of the financial information furnished along with the budget forms.

More affluent families may present a more complex problem. A considerable amount of additional financial information covering the last three years will be required. This would normally include copies of income tax returns, personal financial statements, and financial statements of any business or professional corporations in which one of the parties is a principal.

Typically the couple will not have brought this information to the first mediation session. Therefore, any final agreement on property division must be deferred until all information is presented and checked by the mediator to see if assets have been omitted from the current financial statement. Complex problems might arise over valuation of marital properties, in particular such things as partially vested pension or retirement plans.

When family holdings are very substantial and the marriage is of long duration, extremely complex financial problems may arise. Instructions for handling such matters are not within the scope of this book. Impartial resource persons may be needed, such as tax consultants, auditors, and appraisers.

Once marital property has been identified, the couple must reach agreement on how it will be divided. As has been mentioned in an earlier chapter, one rationale for division is to start on a 50-50 basis and then determine whether there are reasons why it might be more just to make a different division. If the couple has been able to reach agreement on division of marital property in the second hour, they will be considering support issues in the third and fourth hours. If not, further consideration will be given to marital property in the third hour.

Support

Before the end of the second hour, or in advance of the time when the couple will begin consideration of support, the mediator should determine whether the combined budgets of the parties exceed family income. Without discussing the problem in detail, the couple should be told that the deficit can only be covered in one of two ways: by finding additional income or reducing the budgets.

If this is a problem which will be considered at the next session, the couple should be cautioned not to discuss it between themselves, but to think instead about how each might contribute to the solution. Emphasis is placed on having each party take individual responsibility. They should be told this means thinking about how *your* budget might be reduced or how *you* might produce additional income, and not how the opposite party's budget might be reduced or how that party might produce additional income.

Third through Sixth Hours

Most couples will complete work on division of marital property, support, and custody arrangements during the first four mediation hours. If settlement is not reached, the mediator must consider whether it is useful for the parties to continue negotiating over a particular issue or to declare an impasse. Another option is for the mediator to simply suspend discussions on a particular issue and begin discussions on another. If that is concluded successfully, they can then return to the previous issue.

Checking Progress

Even though only the mediator may declare an impasse during this period of the mediation process, it is important to check regularly with the parties to avoid having them struggle at length with an issue when it is clear they are not making progress. Doing so will prevent frustration and anger which will then make the settlement of other issues more difficult. If mediators continue to deal with an issue on which the parties are making no progress, they begin to reinforce the couple's unwillingness to agree and invite an escalation of hostile feelings. When this happens, the parties will negotiate less effectively and will try to shift responsibility for resolution of the issue to the mediator.

Time Extensions

If by the end of the sixth hour the parties are not in substantial agreement, they must decide with the mediator whether impasse shall be declared on one or more issues or whether it might be productive to extend mediation time beyond ten hours. Most couples decide to extend the time, agreeing to add four or more hours.

When this decision is made, an additional cost deposit must be paid no later than the beginning of the seventh hour. The rule is that if sessions are to be extended, the decision must be made and additional deposit paid while there are four paid hours remaining from the previous deposit. These last four hours would normally be needed by the advisory attorney after agreement on all issues has been reached.

Seventh Hour

Assuming that the parties have reached agreement on all issues during the first six hours, they will meet with the advisory attorney for the first time during the seventh hour. Mediators summarize for the attorney the agreements reached by the couple, asking the parties to correct them if they make any incorrect statements. Except in more complex situations, an attorney can understand the settlement agreement reached by the parties in one hour.

If legal questions came up during the first six hours which were deferred for the attorney's advice, they may be presented now. Because legal questions are not always predictable, it is preferable for the attorney to come in at the beginning of two scheduled hours. If there are a number of legal questions to be answered, a second hour may be needed. But if the couple and the attorney finish within the first hour, the session may be concluded and the second hour canceled without charge. On the other hand, if there is still a controversy over custody, an additional deposit must be made to cover the mediation time needed for negotiating custody and visitation.

Eighth Hour

Assuming all issues were agreed upon and consultation with the attorney completed during the previous seven hours, the advisory attorney will bring the final settlement agreement to this eighth-hour session. In most instances only minor, if any, changes are required. Normally only one hour will be scheduled for the attorney's presentation of the contract. But if substantial changes are required, a ninth hour may need to be scheduled at which time the corrected agreement will be presented by the advisory attorney. In most instances this will be the final session, following a total of eight hours of mediation time.

Ninth Hour

When custody is in dispute, all financial issues must be resolved and a written agreement signed, leaving open only the question of custody and/or visitation during the ninth hour. Assuming that both must be decided, arrangements regarding visitation for the noncustodial parent will be decided first.

Prior to this session, agreement will have been reached regarding the participation of children in the session. The first effort of mediators at this session is to establish a relationship with them. Mediators can enlist the aid of the parents in helping explain to the children why they are there and what problems must be resolved.

It is important that the *parents* rather than the mediator give the children express permission to say whatever they wish during the mediation sessions. Even if the parents contend they have already said this to the children, it is important that they repeat it now. It is not sufficient for one parent to simply say, "I agree with what your father said." Each must give permission in *his or her own words*. It is also important that the children be given protection. Convincingly stated assurance is needed from each parent that there will be no consequences resulting from whatever the children say.

If the parents go through this process in a ritualistic manner, it will mean little to the children. Mediators must decide whether the parents have actually convinced the children. If there is the slightest uncertainty, and there usually is, a check with the children is indicated, after which further assurances may be offered.

Most children do have a preference about which parent they wish to live with, but do not wish to hurt or seemingly reject the other parent. In the short period of time available in mediation, the children may not be able to resolve this dilemma. If they cannot, neither the mediator nor the parents should force a decision. Generally, their preferences will become apparent in other ways.

It is well for the mediator and the parties to remember that no custody arrangements are ever permanent. All are subject to changes as a result of changing circumstances and preferences. Many options for change are available to the parties, such as agreeing to follow certain custodial arrangements for a year or more. At the end of that time, the arrangement will be reexamined by the parties and the children, and one of three decisions can be made:

1. They can continue the arrangement.
2. They can agree to change it.
3. If they do not agree, they can return for further mediation.

Suggested Readings

Marital Mediation Rules, Appendix FMA-C.
Orientation, Part I, Appendix FMA-A.
Orientation, Part II, Appendix FMA-B.
Forms FMA 177 through FMA 1377, Appendix FMA-G.
Marital Arbitration Rules, Appendix FMA-D.

5 Budgeting

Budgeting is the only rational means of breaking down anticipated expenditures into various categories in order to keep them within the limits of income. Normally, budgeting is a flexible, personal plan that changes as income and long- and short-term goals shift. However, budgeting for a divorce settlement is considerably less flexible. When one family's income must stretch in order to operate two households, ranking expenditures in terms of priorities as well as categories becomes imperative. There is seldom enough income to meet what are considered legitimate needs.

Normally a budget may cover any convenient period of time and be estimated monthly, quarterly, or yearly according to the calendar, school session, or for tax purposes. In divorce, monthly figures and payments are most frequently required. Yearly projections are necessary so that seasonal or periodic income and expenditures can be averaged out.

Role of Mediator

In order to help the couple determine financial arrangements for child support and/or spousal maintenance, the mediator must gain an understanding of the family's previous living expenses and life-style, as well as current needs and expectations. The role of the mediator in helping the couple determine financial settlements is one of reality tester, providing mechanisms for structured, systematic review of available income and necessary expenditures. Careful line itemization and insistence upon factually documented need eliminates guesswork and helps reduce the emotional charge inherent in dividing up the family income.

Many families have no formalized method of handling money. Often one spouse has controlled the family finances, or divisions in responsibilities have resulted in marked ignorance about certain economic areas. Discussions of money can be as much a battleground for power struggles as sex, touching off deep-seated feelings of resentment, helplessness, inadequacy, and rigidity. Some families may be uneasy about disclosing financial matters or uncertain as to how to gather needed information. The mediator should assure the couple of confidentiality and provide as much direction as necessary.

During the orientation session, the mediator gives each spouse the assignment of completing a budget form for him/herself, based upon the estimated cost of living separately. When custody is an issue between the parties, two budgets are requested from each: one with the children's expenses included and one without. This enables the parties to separate their practical financial needs from the emotional issue of who will obtain custody of the children.

The pattern of expenditures will be a reflection of individual preferences and life-styles. Some persons prefer to spend a large portion of their income on housing and skimp on transportation. Some need a large clothing allowance. Some prefer to entertain and travel with their money. No two individuals and no two budgets are alike. The mediator should avoid imposing value judgments on the priorities set by the parties. A good budget and a good settlement are those that can be lived with by the persons involved. Budget forms are included in Appendix FMA-G.

Forms Needed

Most budget formats do not include detailing income, assets, and liabilities; yet these should be listed to provide a complete financial picture. Simplified forms for this information (Form FMA 277) are included in Appendix FMA-G. Under the rules, the mediator must require full financial disclosure by both parties. A financial statement (balance sheet) and profit and loss statement, tax returns, buy-sell agreements, and other documents showing income, assets, and liabilities prepared during the last three years should be furnished by those clients with business interests. Income tax returns and financial statements furnished previously provide the mediator with a basis for comparison and evaluation of thoroughness, and should be required as part of the full disclosure.

Estimating Income

Gross income is the most commonly known figure to both parties and should provide the base for further calculations. Estimated income should begin with annual fixed income. All wages, salaries, social security benefits, tips, pensions, allowances, anticipated support payments, etc., should be included. Any variable income, such as interest from savings, bonds, trusts, dividends from stocks, rentals, gifts, bonuses, profitable hobbies, etc., should be estimated and included for a total annual-income figure.

When earnings are irregular, estimates may be based on previous income and current prospects. If income fluctuates sharply, such as for seasonal workers, sales agents on commission, farmers, the self-employed, etc., two estimates may be necessary: the smallest and largest figures expected. Budgets should be based on the lower figure. It is wiser not to count on optimistic expectations.

Withholding taxes, estimated taxes, insurance, social security, self-employment, pensions, and other deductions may then be subtracted, yielding net income or take-home pay. Mediators must remind clients that present deductions will change after divorce, making estimates of revised deductions necessary. The average monthly family income, after deductions, may then be divided according to budgeted needs.

Estimating Expenses

Often clients do not know where to begin estimating their expenses. The mediator may suggest that clients utilize any existing record of family spending. Checkbook stubs, receipts, and old bills from the past twelve or more months will give a fairly accurate picture of expenditures when they are categorized according to the budget form which will be used. A family expenditures analysis sheet (Form FMA 477), such as is found in Appendix FMA-G, may be used in this way. The mediator must check statements of necessary expenses closely, ensuring that all necessary and applicable figures are included.

Set-asides

Expenditures generally fall into three categories: set-asides, regular monthly expenses, and day-to-day expenses. *Set-asides* are monies earmarked for unplanned and seasonal expenses. These emergency provisions are a cushion for minor crises too small to be covered by insurance, but too large to be absorbed by the monthly expense account, such as blown-out tires or appliance repair. Seasonal expenses include property taxes, car insurance, life insurance, license tags, vacation funds, and similar items (see Form FMA 377B).

Future expenses are also included in set-asides. Major expenditures in which both parties have an interest, such as the children's college education or weddings, can be planned in advance by prorating a small amount each month. The divorcing couple may choose to contribute an equitable proportion of each party's income to such expenditures (see Form FMA 377A). A dollar cost may be assigned to each party and a date set as a deadline for the monies to be available. The monthly figure to set aside may be obtained by dividing the assigned cost by the number of months necessary to reach the goal.

Monthly Expenses

Regular monthly expenses are the easiest to estimate; yet the mediator should be sure that all the following are included:

1. Mortgage payment with real estate taxes and insurance or rent
2. Utilities—heat, electricity, water, telephone, garbage collections, etc.
3. Installment loan payments (see Form FMA 377C)
4. Hospital or health insurance premiums
5. Any other regular, fixed expenses, such as room and board for a child at school, music or dancing lessons, nursery school or day care, pledges or contributions, society or union dues, exterminators, etc.

Discretionary Expenses

After regular expenses are met, the remaining income is discretionary or variable according to preference, circumstance, or need. Expenditures may fluctuate sharply from month to month. Items in this category are the easiest to trim when necessary. Often one spouse or the other has no conception of how much money is needed for items he or she is unaccustomed to buying. The mediator should carefully check the budget to make sure that nothing on the following checklist is forgotten (see Form FMA 377).

Budget Checklist

Food: groceries, meals and snacks eaten away from home, alcohol, soft drinks, school lunches, candy, gum

Clothing: ready-made garments, accessories, fabric and notions for clothing repair, paid storage, dry cleaning, outside laundry fees

Transportation: car, motorcycle, and/or boat gasoline, oil, repair, and maintenance; depreciation allowance; parking fees; bus; train, plane, and taxi fares

Medical Expenses: doctor and dentist bills, hospital and nursing care, health insurance premiums, drugs and medication, eyeglasses, braces

Household supplies: equipment and tools for cooking, laundering, cleaning, yard maintenance, paid domestic services

Furnishings: furniture, appliance replacements, linens, curtains, tableware, rugs, clocks

Personal items: beauty and barbershop services, shaving supplies, cosmetics, stationery and writing supplies, jewelry, tobacco

Education: books, magazines, newspapers; tuition, lessons, dues, other professional expenses such as conferences

Recreation: hobby supplies, toys, birthday parties, babysitting fees, sports equipment, athletic events, movies, film and camera, concerts

Gifts and contributions: Christmas expenses; gifts to individuals, Red Cross, and other charities; church donations

Security plan: stocks, bonds, retirement

Revolving or regular installment loans to department stores, etc.

Comparing Expenses and Income

If the figures from the monthly expenditures balance with the estimated income, the mediator and clients are in luck. If income exceeds expenses, remaining monies may be used for savings, trust funds, meeting more of the parties' immediate goals, and other expenditures. Usually, however, expenses will greatly exceed the income available. The couple may list all possible anticipated expenses as a bargaining strategy or as a way of denying the often realistic necessity of both parties' cutting back their standard of living to some degree. The mediator should confront the couple with these discrepancies and help them reevaluate their needs.

The high percentage of defaults on payments, beginning shortly after the judge makes his or her awards, is a result of the traditional adversarial legal system imposing a settlement on the divorcing client. An individual is much more likely to abide by an agreement which he or she has discussed thoroughly beforehand, which is based on budget information developed *by both parties* and is entered into willingly.

Trimming Expenses

An impartial, third-party facilitator can point out the couple's need to look at priorities, but only the parties themselves can decide what those priorities are. In determining financial settlements, as in other aspects of mediation, the goal is to establish and maintain good communication between the parties. If expenses must be altered to balance available income, the mediator may need to reemphasize the difference between needs and wants. Of course, basic necessities can be justified and validated and should result in few arguments. However, cutting down more flexible expenditures may trigger strong emotional resistance.

Often clients will exaggerate their needs in an attempt to be assured of financial security. The mediator may wish to remind them that by making rational rather than emotional decisions and by accepting the change in circumstances resulting from the divorce, both parties can win. When mediators recognize signs of power struggles, revenge, or agitation in the face of undue rigidity, they may point out these dynamics to the couple and restate their desire to help protect both of them. Compromise is essential in working toward a comfortable arrangement that both parties can live with.

Budget-Balancing Techniques

Clients will often appear to be inflexible about modifying financial needs only because they are not aware of all available options. The mediator should take the responsibility for suggesting alternative solutions which may help to balance the budget. For example, the couple might consider converting to cheaper forms of insurance or consulting with creditors to reduce the amounts of installment payments. Assets could be sold to reduce payments, produce more disposable income, or minimize excess expenditures.

A large family car may no longer be a necessity. Trading for a small less expensive automobile may result in netting cash as well as in more economical gas mileage. Selling the home may lessen unwanted household responsibilities, in addition to increasing available cash and providing the opportunity to move closer to work.

The possibility or necessity of increasing the family income by having the wife take a job should also be explored. Although extra expenses such as day care, lunches, or extra clothing are likely to be incurred, the idea that these expenses will drain a working mother's income until it is without profit is largely untrue. Even $100 extra a month will help meet family expenses. The mediator may need to explore the woman's feelings about her role and the discrepancy between her preferences and reality.

Spousal maintenance can be viewed as a gift of time to allow a woman who has never worked the opportunity to receive the education or training necessary to become self-supporting. Continued dependency on an unwilling spouse is degrading and unrealistic in today's world.

Children can be helped to understand the need for belt tightening and self-support by having the financial situation explained to them. Encouraging their participation through careful money management and odd jobs will not only help the family finances but also reduce fears children may have about the need to economize.

Debts

For the couple with large outstanding debts, a regular plan of payments deducted from each paycheck can often be arranged with employers. Creditors who are informed of a change in circumstances and a sincere desire to systematize debt payment are usually willing to cooperate. Help with handling credit problems may be obtained through county extension agents, credit counseling services, and family service agencies.

A word of caution about consolidation: we recommend that debt consolidation, if considered, be handled by nonprofit organizations only, since these organizations charge no fee to the customer. Loan consolidation companies are illegal in many states, and mediators should familiarize themselves with local laws governing them. Some debt consolidation services charge a high fee and one monthly payment from the client, which they will then supposedly prorate to creditors in reduced amounts. However, often they will be unable to obtain agreement from all creditors or will not even notify them, and may keep the client's money themselves. The client is then made aware of the lack of payments by a very angry creditor or an even more threatening collection agency.

Spending Guidelines

The U.S. Bureau of Labor Statistics tracks spending patterns of families throughout the United States. Periodic reports published by the bureau may be obtained through regional offices. Tables 5-1, 5-2, and 5-3 represent cost estimates for a family of four during autumn 1975. The family includes a 38-year-old husband employed full time, his wife who is not working, and two children—a boy of 13 and a girl of 8. Nothing has been included for savings. These statistics are listed here only as a comparative guide for those couples or the mediator interested in national averages. The listing should not be considered a working blueprint. Personal and cultural preferences influence a family's spending habits and choices. The needs of children will vary, depending on age, and may increase living costs while income remains stable.

The amount of money available to the family, or their level of income, will itself influence the percentage of monies spent on various items in the budget. For example, a family on a modest budget will spend proportionately more of their total income on food, rent, medical care, transportation, and other necessities than will a family with more resources. Geographical area of residence also influences spending patterns. The cost of living is much higher in Hawaii, Alaska, Washington, D.C., New York, and other major industrial cities than it is in the South or other regions of the country. Equivalence scales which adjust the demographic composition of the family in the Cost-of-Living Index may be obtained from the Bureau of Labor.

Many couples will ask for guidelines to follow or check with to give them some reassurance in reaching settlement. Some courts and other agencies have prepared guides which are not intended to be used literally, realizing that the needs and life-styles of families vary widely. With the caution that these are only very general guides, two examples are included at the end of this chapter—one from Marin County, California, and the other from Cobb County, Georgia (see tables 5-4, 5-5, and 5-6 at end of chapter).

With changing circumstances and the passing of time, families may discover a need to reevaluate their original settlement agreement. The mediator should encourage families to return to mediation in order to make the needed alterations in their budget plans.

Suggested Readings

See Bibliography for complete references

Books

Auerbach, *Your Money—How to Make It Stretch.*
Blodgett, *The New York Times Book of Money.*
Hurley, *Personal Money Management.*
J.K. Lasser Institute, *Managing Your Family Finances.*

Pamphlets

U.S. Department of Agriculture, *A Guide to Budgeting for the Family.*
U.S. Department of Agriculture, *Family Economics Review.* A quarterly report on research of the Consumer and Food Economics Institute and on information from other sources relating to economic aspects of family living, such as health insurance, clothing budgets, costs of food, energy prices, etc.
U.S. Department of Labor, *The Consumer Price Index.* A statistical measure of changes in prices of goods and services bought by urban wage earners and clerical workers, including families and single persons. CPI—A Short Description, 1974-620-171/2352 3-1, is also available to explain the index measurement.
U.S. Department of Labor, *A Guide to Living Costs.*
U.S. Department of Labor, *Three Standards of Living.*

Table 5-1
Lower-Income Budget, Family of Four, Southeastern United States

	Annual	Monthly	Percent
Food (at home and away)	$2952	$246	30.7
Rent	1391	116	14.5
House furnishing and operations	467	39	4.8
Transportation (auto owners)	939	78	9.7
Clothing	771	64	8.0
Personal care	248	20	2.5
Medical care	818	68	8.5
Other consumption[a]	447	37	4.6
Social security	577	48	6.0
Income taxes	781	65	8.1
(Miscellaneous)	436	36	4.5
Total	$9588	$799	100%

Source: U.S. Department of Commerce, National Technical Information Service, *Three Standards of Living for an Urban Family of Four Persons,* Spring 1967.

Note: These figures are for urban areas in autumn 1975. The average for metropolitan areas was $9720; for nonmetropolitan areas, $9002.

[a]Recreation, education, etc.

Table 5-2
Intermediate-Income Budget, Family of Four, Southeastern United States

	Annual	Monthly	Percent
Food (at home and away)	$ 3827	$ 319	24.9
Rent or	1802	150	11.7
Mortgage	3048	254	17.6
House furnishing and operations	797	66	5.2
Transportation (auto owners)	1342	112	8.7
Clothing	1102	92	7.19
Personal care	331	28	2.1
Medical care	882	73	5.3
Other consumption[a]	831	69	5.4
Social security	834	69	5.4
Income taxes	2057	171	13.4
Miscellaneous	701	58	4.5
Total	$15,318	$1276	100%

Source: U.S. Department of Commerce, National Technical Information Service, *Three Standards of Living for an Urban Family of Four Persons,* Spring 1967.

Note: These figures are for urban areas in autumn 1975. The average for metropolitan areas was $15,363; for nonmetropolitan areas, $13,886.

[a]Recreation, education, etc.

Table 5-3

Higher-Income Budget, Family of Four, Southeastern United States

	Annual	Monthly	Percent
Food (at home and away)	$4819	$402	21.6
Rent or	2843	237	12.7
Mortgage	3836	319	17.2
House furnishings and operations	1508	126	6.7
Transportation (auto owners)	1658	138	7.4
Clothing	1613	134	7.2
Personal care	470	39	2.1
Medical care	857	71	3.8
Other consumption[a]	1371	114	6.1
Social security	841	70	3.7
Income taxes	4130	344	18.5
Miscellaneous	1182	98	5.3
Total	$22,294	$1897	100%

Source: U.S. Department of Commerce, National Technical Information Service, *Three Standards of Living for an Urban Family of Four Persons,* Spring 1967.

Note: These figures are for urban areas in autumn 1975. The average for metropolitan areas was $22,940; for nonmetropolitan areas, $19,412.

[a]Recreation, education, etc.

Table 5-4

Guidelines for Temporary Support in Domestic Cases, Cobb County, Georgia

Net Monthly Income	Spouse Alone	Child Support Only	Spouse and One Child	Spouse and Two Children	Spouse and Three or More Children
$ 200	$ 50	$50-75	$ 50-75	$ 50-75	$ 50-75
250	50	50-75	50-75	65-75	65-75
300	75	50-75	100	100	100
350	100	50-75	125	125	125
400	150	50-75	150	150	150
500	200	75-100	200	200	200
600	250	75-100	300	300	300
700	300	75-100	350	375	400
800	235	125-150	375	425	450
900	350	125-150	425	475	500
1000	400	150-175	475	525	550
1200	475	150-175	550	625	650
1400	550	175-200	650	725	775
1600	625	175-200	700	800	875
1800	700	200-250	775	900	1000
2000	775	200-250	875	100	1100

Source: Superior Court of Cobb County, Georgia.

Table 5-4 (continued)

Net monthly income means after deducting federal and state income taxes, social security, employee tax, health insurance for dependents, union dues, retirement or pension fund. If income lies somewhere between the figures used, the court may average the difference.

Spouse alone: If wife is working, generally no spousal support will be allowed if her income is over 60 percent of her husband's. If it is less than 60 percent, one-half her earnings will be deducted from spousal support.

If children are under school age, wife will generally not be required to work.

Handicapped wife or children are usually given special consideration.

Prior marriages: Consideration will be given to reasonable expenses for children of former marriages in spouse's custody, payments of support orders re prior marriages, and reasonable child care expenses paid by working custodial parent.

Table 5-5
Schedule for Child Support Payments where No Spousal Support Is Ordered, Marin County, California

Noncustodial Parent's Net Monthly Income[a]	One Child	Two Children	Three or More Children
$ 400	$100	$100	$100
500	125	150	175
600	150	200	225
700	150	250	275
800	150	250	300
900	175	275	350
1000	175	300	375
1200	200	350	450
1400	250	400	525
1600	250	450	600
1800	275	500	675
2000	300	550	750
Above 2000	Court's discretion		

Source: Superior Court of Marin County, California.

Notes: This schedule is prepared with the assumption that the custodial parent's net earnings are at least 25 percent less than that of the noncustodial parent and that there is no award of spousal support.

The rule for support is intended to be the same whether the custodial parent is the father or the mother.

If the noncustodial parent carries hospital, medical, or dental insurance covering the children, the cost attributable to the children's coverage may be deducted from the support payments.

[a]Income after compulsory deductions such as income tax, FICA, SDI, and compulsory retirement.

Table 5-6

Guidelines for Duration of Spousal Support after Dissolution or Legal Separation, Marin County, California

Length of Marriage	Duration of Support
Under 12 years	It is presumed that spousal support shall terminate after a period equivalent to one-half the duration of the marriage.
12 to 15 years	There is no presumption for termination of spousal support. The following factors to be considered (whether or not it shall terminate): wife's education, training, work experience, health and age; husband's ability to pay support; wife's eligibility for social security.[a]
Over 25 years	It is presumed that permanent spousal support shall not terminate unless wife remarries.

1. Presence or absence of preschool children to be considered if husband has income above minimum.

2. Special consideration to be given to the ill health of either spouse.

3. After 25 years of marriage, the wife is presumed to require spousal support.

4. Duration of temporary spousal support payments should be taken into account.

Amount of Spousal Support

If the *net* earnings of one spouse are $300 to $600, *maximum* support to the other spouse is one-third of that income.

If the *net* earnings of one spouse are over $600, *maximum* support to the other spouse shall not exceed 40 percent of that amount.

If there is both spousal and child support, the combined order should not exceed 50 percent of the supporting spouse's net income.

No spousal support shall be provided to any spouse who, following dissolution, has income sufficient to maintain his or her standard of living.

Source: Superior Court of Marin County, California.

[a]Current social security regulations (42 U.S.C. 402b) provide that a wife divorced after 20 years of marriage is entitled to social security benefits.

6 Tax Considerations

When a couple has made the decision to separate and form two separate households, the bulk of the remaining discussions will center on the division of marital assets, support payments for minor children and possibly one spouse, and a settlement of property rights. It is a good idea to keep in mind during these discussions that there is a third party interested in the results, even though not present in the discussions—the Internal Revenue Service. There are tax ramifications to a separation agreement which should be considered before the agreement is put in final form. The 1976 Tax Reform Act brought about several changes in the tax laws which directly affect divorced or separated taxpayers. In order to avoid confusion, this chapter will deal with the law as it now stands rather than compare the old law with the new.

Child Support

Statute and case law require the support of children throughout their minority. The age of majority, most frequently age 18, is fixed by state laws and varies from state to state. In most states, the mother may be required to share support of minor children with the father. Support by law includes necessities such as food, clothing, shelter, and education. This obligation can often be enforced through criminal proceedings. Therefore, child support is an important item of any separation agreement where the parties have minor children.

If the mother is to be the custodial parent, as is the usual case, the father will be required to pay a fixed sum on a regular basis for the support of each minor child. Payments which are clearly defined as child support will not be deductible from the taxable income of the father, nor can they be included as taxable income of the mother or the minor children. To fit into the classification of child support, however, the payments must be *unequivocally designated* as child support in the agreement or divorce decree. An amount which is to be paid by the husband for the support of both the wife and children will probably be characterized entirely as alimony, with different tax consequences to the parties.

If the parties have calculated the tax consequences as part of the process in arriving at a figure for family support, it may be to the advantage of both parties that the spousal maintenance and child support be comingled in such a way as to make the entire sum paid by the husband deductible to him and taxable to the wife.

Support of Spouse

The terms *alimony* and *spousal maintenance* or *spousal support* have somewhat different meanings but are frequently used interchangeably. For tax purposes no distinction is made, and spousal maintenance will be treated as alimony. According to tax law, money going from one spouse to another in a divorce setting is one of two things: it is either alimony or a property settlement payment.

Alimony or Property Settlement?

If the money is characterized as alimony, it will be deductible to the one who pays it and taxable to the one who receives it. On the other hand, if the money is characterized as a property settlement payment, it is neither deductible to the payer nor taxable to the recipient. It is important for the couple and the mediator to be aware of these consequences and to structure the agreement so that it provides the most beneficial tax consequences to both parties.

A series of payments will be classified as alimony if certain conditions are met. First, the payments must be incident to a document. This document may be an actual decree of divorce or separate maintenance, a written instrument incident to a divorce or separation, a separation agreement, or a decree of support. The second requirement for alimony to be deductible is that the payments must be periodic and not payments on a principal sum. Payments will be deemed to be periodic if they are subject to a contingency, such as the death of either spouse, the remarriage of the wife, or a change in the economic status of either spouse.

Combining Spouse and Child Support

In a situation where the husband will be paying a sum to the wife for her support as well as for the support of the minor children, the agreement can be written in such a manner that the entire amount he is obligated to pay, including support of the children, will be deductible to him and taxable to her. It is quite possible that doing so will provide more disposable income to each party than designating part as alimony and part as child support.

To illustrate, assume the husband has an income of $100,000 and deductions of $20,000 per year. The wife has no independent income and will have deductions (interest, taxes, medical expenses, etc., and one exemption) of $5750. There are three minor children. The couple has calculated that the wife needs $31,000 per year for herself and the children.

Child Support Only. If $31,000 is designated as child support only, the resulting tax consequences are shown in table 6-1.

Child Support and Alimony. If $15,000 is designated as child support and an adjustment is made so that the wife will have net alimony after taxes of $16,000 (the actual amount of alimony must be increased to $19,000) the tax consequences are as shown in table 6-2.

Alimony Only. If all the wife's income is characterized as alimony, it would be necessary for her to receive $44,000 in order to net $31,000. See table 6-3.

Summary. Table 6-4 summarizes all the preceding data.

Admittedly, not many couples will be in these tax brackets, but the same principles apply in lower income brackets as well. Before an informed decision can be made in any situation, it is essential to calculate the consequences with the particular facts and figures of the couple.

In those situations where there are no children and consequently no child support is paid, it is still important to calculate the tax consequences of alimony. If the husband has agreed to pay an amount of alimony to the wife based on a budget of her needs, she will not have the full amount for

Table 6-1
Tax Consequences of Only Child Support

Husband			
Gross income	$100,000	Gross income	$100,000
Deductions	−20,000	Child support	−31,000
Taxable income	80,000	Remaining income	69,000
Tax	39,390	Taxes	−39,390
		Disposable income	29,610

Wife			
Child-support	31,000		
Deductions[a]	0		
Tax	0		
Disposable income	31,000		

[a]The wife will have no use for any available deductions, since she has no taxable income.

Table 6-2
Tax Consequences of Child Support and Alimony

	Husband		
Gross income	$100,000	Gross income	$100,000
Deductions	−20,000	Child support	−15,000
	80,000		85,000
Alimony deduction	−19,000	Alimony	−19,000
Taxable income	61,000		66,000
Tax	26,890	Taxes	−26,890
		Disposable income	39,110

	Wife		
Income (alimony)	$19,000	Alimony	$ 19,000
Deductions	−5,750	Child support	+15,000
Taxable income	13,250	Gross income	34,000
Tax	2,777	Taxes	−2,777
		Disposable income	$31,223

expenses because she must also pay income tax. The husband will need to increase the amount of alimony and include taxes if the parties have agreed that the wife needs a certain amount of disposable income. While the husband will certainly be out-of-pocket more, it may ease the pain for him to see his taxes decrease as a result of his increased deduction.

Table 6-3
Tax Consequences of Only Alimony

	Husband		
Gross income	$100,000	Gross income	$100,000
Deductions	−20,000	Alimony	−44,000
	80,000		56,000
Alimony deduction	−44,000	Taxes	−12,290
Taxable income	36,000	Disposable income	43,710
Tax	12,290		

	Wife		
Income (alimony)	$ 44,000	Gross income	$ 44,000
Deductions	−5,750	Tax	−12,365
Taxable income	38,250	Disposable income	31,365
Tax	12,365		

Table 6-4
Tax Consequences—A Summary

	All Child Support	Child Support and Alimony	All Alimony
Taxes paid by husband	$39,390	$26,890	$12,290
Taxes paid by wife	+0	+2,777	+12,365
Total taxes	39,390	29,667	24,655
Husband's disposable income	29,610	39,110	43,710
Wife's disposable income	$31,000	$31,223	$31,635

Note: The tax calculations on the husband's income do not take into account the 50 percent maximum tax on earned income. While this tax provision may lower the total tax due from the husband, it would not affect the basic principles here.

The wife should also be made cognizant of the fact that she should file quarterly estimated-tax returns because she is receiving taxable income that is not subject to withholding. The local IRS office can supply the necessary forms and instruction pamphlet. The returns are due April 15, June 15, September 15, and January 15 for each calendar year.

It should also be noted that no deduction is allowed a husband for voluntary payments that are not made pursuant to a document. For that reason, it is important to get a temporary agreement in writing as soon as feasible after mediation has begun. The same rule applies to additional voluntary payments made after the divorce.

Property Settlement

When a couple decides to separate and establish two households, there must be some physical division of property acquired during the term of the marriage. When there are substantial assets to divide, such as real property or securities, there may be tax consequences as well, particularly if the assets have changed significantly in value since they were acquired.

Transferring Property

As a general rule, if the husband transfers appreciated property to the wife as part of the property settlement, he is subject to tax on the difference between his cost basis and the value of the property at the time of transfer. If the asset itself is a capital asset, the difference will be taxed at capital-gains rates. The theory behind this tax rests on the idea that a wife, by law, has certain marital claims to the husband's estate and these claims are being "bought" by the husband with the transferred property. The value of her rights is the fair market value of the property she receives, so her basis will be the value at the time of transfer.

The most typical transfers are probably furniture and automobiles. Since these items usually depreciate from their original basis, there would be no tax as a result of the transfer. The husband would not be entitled to take a loss deduction, since these items are personal property and are neither business property nor capital assets.

Another typical transfer is the home. If the home is in the husband's name and he transfers it to the wife under the terms of the settlement agreement, he will be subject to a capital-gains tax if the home has increased in value. Of course, if he and the wife have joint title to the home as tenants-in-common, then the tax would be computed on one-half of the gain, because the husband is only transferring one-half of the property.

Paying in Installments

Another possible settlement of property rights is for the husband to agree to pay the wife a principal sum in installments over a period of time. In order to qualify as a principal sum, the amount must be payable in all events. If it is subject to any usual contingency (i.e., remarriage of the wife, death of either party), then the payments will be classified as alimony. If the payments are not subject to any contingencies and can be stated in a definite amount, they will not be deductible to the husband nor taxable to the wife, with one noteworthy exception. If these payments extend over a period ending more than ten years from the date of the decree, instrument, or agreement, then the husband will be able to deduct his annual payments each year up to a maximum of 10 percent of the principal amount.

For example, the husband agrees to pay the wife $36,000 over a fifteen-year period. He pays $5000 for the first year, $5000 the second year, and $2000 per year for the remaining thirteen years. His deduction for the first and second year is limited to $3600, or 10 percent of the total each year. He will be able to deduct the full $2000 for the remaining thirteen years, because each of those payments is less than 10 percent of the total amount. As with the other areas of divorce law, if the husband deducts it, the wife must include it in her gross income.

Filing Status

The amount of tax to be paid on any given amount of taxable income will depend on the filing status of the taxpayer as of December 31. There are four possible filing statuses: unmarried, married-joint, married-separate, and head of household. As in any tax situation where there is more than one option, the tax consequences should be worked out before an option is finally selected.

Married-Joint

The least tax will be paid on married-joint returns. A couple may file a joint return even if they were separated on December 31, as long as no decree of divorce or separate maintenance has been entered. However, if one spouse has been paying alimony under a separation agreement, the alimony may not be deducted from a joint return.

Head of Household

The next best status is head of household. A taxpayer normally qualifies as head of household only if he/she is not married on December 31 and provides the principal home for certain family members. The custodial parents will normally qualify as head of household, even if they do not claim the children as dependents. A woman may also qualify as head of household even while married, if she provides the principal home for the children during the year, her spouse has lived away from home for the entire taxable year, and she files a separate return. The husband, however, must still file as married-separate and not as a single individual. (Taxpayers who are not married on December 31 and provide a home only for themselves file a return as a single individual.)

Married-Separate

The highest rates are applied to married-separate returns. This rate structure must be used if two married persons elect not to file a joint return. The separate return is necessary in order for the husband to deduct alimony he has paid under a separate agreement, but the couple will rarely save total tax dollars by filing separate returns. Furthermore, if one spouse itemizes deductions, the other spouse must also, even though the standard deduction would be more advantageous.

Exemption for Minor Children

Another issue to be resolved in a divorce situation where there are minor children is the dependency exemption. There has been a great deal of litigation in this area of tax law. It is much better for the parties to resolve this matter in mediation than to leave it unsettled or unconsidered. Under current law, the party who claims the child will be able to reduce his or her taxable income by $750 for each child claimed. This is true whether the taxpayer itemizes deductions or takes the standard deduction. The tax benefit will vary, of course, with the tax bracket of the taxpayer.

For example, assume a divorced couple has two minor children. The father has a taxable income for the year of $10,000, and the mother has a taxable income that year of $5,000. The tax for a single individual on $10,000 is $2090. If the father claims both children, his taxable income will be reduced to $8500 ($10,000 − $1500, or $750 × 2) and his tax reduced to $1,715. Tax on $5000 for the head of the household (for which the mother would qualify if the children were living with her) is $850. The tax on an income of $3500 ($5000 − $1500, or $750 × 2) would be $570.

While the exemptions would be valuable to either, they will be more valuable to the spouse with the higher income, who is usually the father. The premise underlying the exemption is that the one who provides over 50 percent of the support is entitled to it. In order to reduce the problems which can arise in determining the fact, the tax law creates a series of presumptions.

Legal Presumptions

First, if there is no separation agreement, tax law presumes that the custodial parent is entitled to the dependency exemptions. However, if the separation agreement gives the exemption to the noncustodial parent and that parent pays at least $600 per year as child support for each child claimed, then there is a presumption that the noncustodial parent is entitled to the exemptions.

The presumption stays with the custodial parent, unless the agreement provides otherwise or the noncustodial parent has provided at least $1200 per year per child for child support. If he has, then he is entitled to the exemption, unless the custodial parent can clearly show that she has contributed more toward the support of the children than the noncustodial parent. The amounts paid by the noncustodial parent are applied first to the child's expense. The balance is assumed to have been paid by the custodial parent.

Example

Let us suppose that the father pays $100 per month child support for one child and the mother can show she spent a total of $2200 during the year for the child:

Total expenses	$2200
Father's contribution	1200
Mother's contribution	$1000

In this case, the father is entitled to the exemption.

Suppose, however, that the total expenses for the child are $2500:

Total expenses	$2500
Father's contribution	1200
Mother's contribution	$1300

In this case, the mother would be entitled to the exemption.

If there is a separation agreement which includes a designation of dependency exemptions for the children, it will be followed by IRS if the exemptions are allocated to the noncustodial parent and he actually pays at least $600 per year per child. It should be noted that a noncustodial parent who pays at least $1200 per year per child may claim the children as exemptions in spite of a designation to the contrary in an agreement, unless the custodial parent can clearly establish that she contributed more than 50 percent of the child's expenses during the year.

Child-Care Expense Credit

The parent having custody of the children the longer part of the year is entitled to a credit for child-care expenses. This is true whether or not the parent also claims the child as a dependency exemption. The credit is 20 percent of actual expenses up to $2000 in the case of one child and $4000 for two or more children.

Since the tax benefit is in the form of a credit, the custodial parent may claim the credit and also take the standard deduction. When the tax law provides a credit, it means that *the taxpayer can actually subtract the amount of the credit from the tax due.* The credit offsets taxes dollar for dollar. A deduction, on the other hand, is only subtracted from income *before* the tax is calculated. It does not reduce taxes dollar for dollar.

Medical-Expense Deductions

For the Wife

As long as the couple remains married, the husband may continue to deduct medical expenses paid for the wife along with his own medical expenses. Once the couple is divorced, any medical expenses, including health insurance premiums which the husband is required to pay for the wife, would be deductible by him as alimony as long as the other requirements of alimony are met—i.e., that the payments extend longer than ten years or are subject to a contingency. Of course, any medical expenses which the husband deducts as alimony would be taxable to the wife. But she, in turn, could deduct the expenses herself as medical expenses subject to the limitations of medical deductions in general.

For the Children

If the husband pays the children's medical expenses, he will not be able to deduct these expenses unless he also claims the children as dependency exemptions. Otherwise, medical-expense payments by him are considered the same as other child support payments.

Estate Tax Consequences

In those situations where the husband's estate is obligated to make payments to an ex-wife and/or children, the question arises as to whether these payments will be deductible by the estate for estate tax purposes. They will be if the agreement has been made the order of the court, and if the court has the authority to accept, reject, or materially modify the agreement. The court's authority is a matter of state law.

If the payments are made pursuant to an agreement which has *not* been incorporated into a court order, then the payments will be deductible only if they are made in consideration for the relinquishment of *support* rights. If the payments are made for the relinquishment of *property* rights, they are not deductible.

If the husband is required to maintain insurance on his life payable to his wife, the amount of the insurance proceeds will be includable as assets in his estate. However, if the agreement has been incorporated into a decree in a state where the court has the power and authority to modify or reject the agreement, the amount of the proceeds may be deductible (*not* included as assets) by the estate as an indebtedness in the respect of property included in the gross estate.

7

The Marital Settlement Agreement

Purpose of the Agreement

The ultimate objective of the mediation process is for parties to reach an agreement so that they may avoid having to live with conditions imposed on them by either a court or an arbitrator. Not only research findings, mentioned in chapter 8, but also courts recognize that an agreement reached by husband and wife is much preferred over a court-directed arrangement.

Even a superficial inspection of the results of matrimonial law suits would suggest that parties disposed to solve the economic consequences of marital failure can reach better resolution for themselves than the court can possibly do for them; and they should be encouraged in this direction where the possibility of agreement exists.[1]

Misunderstandings

Despite the wide usage of settlement agreements in matrimonial matters, no published works have been found which do more than explore the legal intricacies of the agreement. In virtually all the suggested contract provisions, there is an implicit assumption that each party will, if possible, violate the agreement. Detailed wording is aimed at anticipating every means by which the agreement may be violated and undertakes to prevent this by adding more words. This approach invites a game called "Finding a Loophole They Overlooked."

Legalistic provisions for support of a spouse or children place the parties in a relationship in which one seems to say to the other, "You pay support only because the contract says you must." For the supporting spouse, this is demeaning. He is deprived of any recognition that he has assumed the support obligation because of his sense of responsibility, decency, and caring. At the same time, the dependent spouse may mistakenly believe that no volition is involved in making the support payments. Thus the dependent spouse may neither feel nor express appreciation for the effort and personal sacrifices the supporting spouse is making. Little wonder, then, that payments often stop, and efforts at collection are unsuccessful.

63

Other Problems

Unlike other civil contracts, the settlement agreement and the marriage contract are three-party agreements with the state as a silent, powerful, and rather enigmatic third party. The marriage and divorce laws are different in each of the fifty states and subject to frequent changes in all of them. Thus a couple's marriage contract under state law has little likelihood of remaining constant throughout a marriage. In Canada each province had its own divorce laws until 1968 when a uniform law was adopted for the entire country. However, efforts since 1903 in the United States to enact a nationally uniform marriage and divorce law have been unsuccessful.

It is a formidable challenge to develop an agreement which fosters self-respect as well as respect for the other party, defines their new relationship, and meets the requirements of the state of residence. Besides, the wording of a settlement agreement must be clear. Unlike most civil contracts, it is one which, in a sense, replaces the marriage contract that has been dissolved. Indeed, if the marriage contract had been negotiated in the same way, there might have been either no marriage or perhaps a better one, depending upon how agreement was reached.

Few would argue that today's style of settlement agreements does not come near to meeting this challenge. In suggesting that a new style of agreement is worth striving for, some will say that this idea is too idealistic or does not accept human nature the way it is. They would agree with the person who said, "If a couple can agree on alimony, they are too compatible to be getting a divorce." Such critics appear to believe that complex, so-called airtight agreements will ensure compliance through court enforcement.

But experience suggests otherwise. It has been demonstrated in case after case that when parties are unwilling to comply with an agreement, they find a way to frustrate enforcement. If a support agreement is to be honored over time, there must be willingness to pay and an understanding of that willingness on the part of the party receiving support.

Need for Change

The development of a new generation of settlement agreements is worthy of an in-depth research project. A new style of agreement is needed in order to implement cooperative settlement procedures. Agreements reached in this way are rooted in mutual acceptance by both parties. Marital mediation has as its goal such cooperatively reached agreements.

A new kind of agreement respecting each party and anticipating cooperation would help the divorced couple establish a new, separate relationship which has the following characteristics:

Each party supports the other's right to choose his or her own lifestyle.

Both parties share parenting responsibilities, including financial support, as fully as possible.

Each party becomes financially independent of the other's support payments as soon as possible. (This does not apply to payments purposely deferred for tax purposes.)

Each party accepts an equal share of the usual life-style reduction which follows the establishment of two households in place of one.

Each party receives a fair share of marital property. This means a division which is most likely to benefit the family.

Each party respects the other's privacy, but as long as they share parental responsibilities, information concerning those activities which affect the lives of the children should be freely exchanged. This must be done directly and not through the children.

As work is done toward the development of a more enlightened settlement agreement, one must be mindful of the requirements of the state as a third party. Consequently, the drafting of a settlement agreement requires technical skill and wording. It can still be drafted so that it is easily understood and reflects the wishes of the husband and wife. Too often the lawyer has dictated the terms of the agreement to the client. Witness the advice of Marvin A. Freeman, judge of the superior court in Los Angeles County, California:

No lawyer should assume that he can sit down and draft a marital settlement agreement on the basis of his understanding of general contract law. The lawyer must become familiar with the substantive aspects of marital settlements. *With respect to this kind of agreement he is more parent than obstetrician.*[2]

Terms of Agreement

The agreement begins with a heading such as "Settlement Agreement." When an action is pending in court, reference should be made to it by the names of the parties and case number. Next come the recitals or "whereas" provisions: date of the agreement, names of parties and children, residence of the parties, time and place of marriage, date of separation, and the consideration which is essential for the validity of every contract. Mutual promises—such as the promise of each to live separately from the other—constitute what lawyers call *consideration.*

Provisions

The following is a description of the provisions usually found in marital settlement agreements. A more comprehensive guide and checklist is in Appendix FMA-F.

Right to Live Separately. The parties agree that they shall continue to live separate and apart for the rest of their lives as though unmarried. However, this provision does not condone adultery.

No Molestation. The parties shall not molest nor interfere with each other, nor attempt to compel cohabitation.

Debts. In the event husband or wife are indebted to each other, agreement must be reached as to payment.

Personal Property. If one party is to remain in the residence, a schedule may be agreed upon as to what property the other will remove and when it will be removed. This refers to such things as household furniture and furnishings, automobiles, and the like.

Real Property. This means land and anything permanently attached to it, such as a house. Fixtures permanently installed in the house are considered a part of the real estate. Permanent fixtures are such things as heating and air-conditioning equipment, hot-water heaters, dishwashers, and the like. Washing machines, electric refrigerators, or dryers which can simply be unplugged are not considered permanent fixtures.

Real Estate or Real Property. The ways in which real estate can be divided should be dictated by family needs. In meeting these needs, a number of options are available.

1. The property can be conveyed outright from one party to another.
2. A partial interest, such as a half interest, in the property can be conveyed from one party to the other. Under a condition of joint ownership, provisions may or may not be included so that, in case of a death, the surviving party shall automatically receive full ownership.
3. Title may be in either or both parties' names or in the children's names, with one party having the right to use the property for a period of years.

Custody. The usual form of custody is that one parent is the custodial parent and the other is the noncustodial parent. (Note the definition in the mediation rules.) Visitation arrangements and cooperation between the parents may still be such that there is substantially a condition of shared custody. Occasionally there is so-called split custody, which means that some children go to one parent as custodial parent and some the other. Joint custody, an option under section 36 of the rules, is an arrangement in which neither parent is designated as custodial parent, so that both parents have equal rights as custodial parents. Increasing numbers of parents are asking for this kind of custodial arrangement.

Child Support. While in many states the legal obligation for child support ends when the child is 18, it is possible and often necessary for parents to contract for support beyond that age. Support will be terminated upon the child's death or other stipulated events, such as attaining a certain age, getting married, leaving school, becoming employed, or entering military service. It is essential that the amount of payment and the dates upon which it is payable be clearly stated. Events which might justify increase, reduction, or temporary suspension of support payments must also be agreed upon.

Spousal Maintenance. If no spousal maintenance is to be paid, this must be specified. When payable, the due date and amount of each payment must be clearly stated. Events which might cause the amount of maintenance to change or terminate must be specified. The most usual is remarriage. In some instances, the amount of maintenance received may be so substantial as to discourage remarriage of the former wife. In such cases, the husband may choose not only to continue alimony for a limited time after remarriage, but to increase the amount or provide a bonus payment as an inducement for remarriage.

Security. In some instances, depending on the husband's financial condition, the parties may agree upon his placing certain assets in trust or under some other form of encumbrance as a guarantee of the continuance of support payments. Such an arrangement need not be taken as evidence of distrust, but rather as a means of protecting such assets from the claims of his creditors.

Life Insurance. Arrangements must be made to continue life insurance for the same reasons it would have been continued had the marriage not been dissolved. If the life insurance is on the life of the husband or the wife, they may wish to designate the children as beneficiaries rather than the opposite spouse. However, if the children are minors, as is usually the case, this has certain disadvantages since the life insurance proceeds would then have to be managed under a guardianship. It is a healthy expression of trust when a spouse is willing to designate the other as beneficiary of his or her insurance, at least while the children are minors.

Health Insurance. Today's cost of major medical bills, dental bills, and hospitalization are such that it is imprudent for most families not to have such coverage. If the family has been covered under such insurance during the marriage, it can be continued for the children but usually not for the former spouse. After the dissolution, each spouse must therefore arrange for his or her own health insurance. The agreement must indicate how coverage will be provided for all family members.

Escalation. Because of the recent rapid rate of inflation, couples sometimes ask for provisions which will automatically increase support payments under certain conditions. Some agreements provide for automatic increases based upon the U.S. Department of Labor Cost-of-Living Index. This may realistically indicate an increased need on the part of the children, but does not indicate that the supporting spouse is earning proportionately more. Moreover, the supporting spouse's cost of living will have increased also.

Another arrangement is to relate increases or decreases to the supporting spouse's income, so that changes in income will result in changes in the level of support payments. But because changes are not related to the needs of the children or spouse, they may prove to be quite unrealistic.

For these reasons changes in support payments should be based on needs as well as ability to pay, derived from *current* information. As circumstances change, the parties can reach further agreements modifying support. If they cannot reach agreement, they can resolve their differences by mediation or arbitration. Provisions for future revisions are preferable to provisions for automatic changes.

Tax Matters. Since an entire chapter in this book has been devoted to tax matters, it is evident that they must be considered in reaching all settlement agreements. The general objective is to maximize tax advantages for the family. Even though the couple is divorced, there is little point in the family as a whole paying more taxes than absolutely necessary.

Testimentary Disposition. Generally, without some testimentary provision in a will, support payments are terminated by death. But it is possible for the parties to agree to make wills containing certain provisions regarding each other or the children. If the estate of either party is substantial, a contract to leave a certain proportion of the estate to the children as a part of the settlement may have the effect of placing the children in the position of creditors of the estate rather than beneficiaries, thus reducing the adjusted gross estate. In some cases this may have a significant impact on liability for estate taxes.

Attorney's Fees. In most states, the wife has the right to recover attorney's fees from the husband. An agreement should be reached regarding this right.

Representations and Warranties. The basis for future modification of the agreement must be predicted on a change of income, needs, or other financial circumstances. It is therefore necessary that the parties warrant the correctness of the income and financial conditions upon which the settlement is based. Another warranty may relate to the division of marital property. It is important that each party list all the property owned at the time of settlement. A later discovery of an undisclosed asset would be a basis for further negotiations or legal action.

Entire Agreement. This provision states that the written contract is the entire agreement and that it is not predicated on any oral promises or other inducements. It will usually be included by the attorney without negotiations on the part of the parties. Its intent is to release them from any and all future claims against each other, including the right to inherit from each other, except as the agreement specifies.

Integration. This provision says that the contract shall remain binding as a civil contract, even though it is included as part of the final judgment and decree. If it is not merged into the decree, it continues its existence as a civil contract, thus affording some rarely used additional legal remedies.

Joint Tax Returns. In cases in which the husband has had most if not all the family income and he prepares and files a joint tax return with his wife, she will wish to have him indemnify her against future assessments against her in connection with these returns.

Disclaimer. In most jurisdictions, parties are not allowed to enter into a contract to get a divorce. Courts hold that public policy affirmatively supports marriage. Divorce is therefore seen as being against marriage. Hence any contract made upon the condition that either party will seek a divorce is void. The disclaimer provision says that no part of the consideration for the settlement agreement is related to either party agreeing to obtain a divorce. Under this provision, neither party is required to obtain a divorce nor is hindered from doing so.

Modification by Mediation. In the event of a need for change in the agreement as a result of changed conditions, or if there should be a dispute regarding its interpretation or application, the parties may agree that such controversies will be resolved in accordance with the Marital Mediation Rules of the Family Mediation Association. Such clauses usually also provide that arbitrations of impasse will be conducted under the Marital Arbitration Rules of the FMA and in accordance with the provisions of state law.

Family Communications. The couple should agree to keep each other informed about all significant events in the lives of the children, such as birthday parties, school plays, honors, sporting events, vacations, prizes, loss of a friend, illnesses, and the like. The parents may also agree that they will keep each other posted as to their own illnesses or other circumstances which may in some way affect the lives of the children.

Model in Appendix

The settlement agreement contained in Appendix FMA-F is not offered as a model form to be followed. It is intended to indicate what such agreements look and sound like. A number of provisions are standard provisions described in the above outline. They may be more or less specific than would be needed in a particular case. Additionally, the model contains a number of fairly unusual provisions which may be included in a contract when circumstances indicate.

Suggested Readings

Stotter, *Drafting the Marital Settlement Agreement.*
Lindey, *Separation Agreements and Ante-Nuptial Contracts. Note*: This is a large two-volume technical work for the legal profession. General familiarity is all that is necessary.

Notes

1. *Shapiro v. Shapiro*, 8 App. 2d 341, 188 N.Y.S.2d 455 (1959).
2. Marvin A. Freeman, "Negotiating Marital Settlement Agreements," in Robert A. Wenke, comp. and ed., *Marital Settlement Agreement Form Book* (Los Angeles: Richter Law Book Co., 1969), p. 1.

8 Arbitration

Arbitration is a means of resolving an impasse reached by parties during their efforts to settle a controversy. In mediation and conciliation, the parties retain the right of deciding. But when impasse is reached, no mutual decision is possible. Consequently, the right to decide must be given to a neutral third party—an arbitrator. Like judges, arbitrators have the power of decision, and the parties compete with each other for a decision in their favor. Thus a competitive win-or-lose view of the proceedings is possible. The parties in arbitration may be represented by attorney advocates, or they may represent themselves.

Advantages of Arbitration

While it is like the adversarial legal system in some respects, arbitration has very clear advantages:

1. *In arbitration,* only the issues in impasse will be decided by the arbitrator. *In court,* while it is possible for the parties to stipulate certain agreements in matrimonial cases, the court will not allow the parties to limit the scope of its decision. In all cases the judge has broadly defined discretion.
2. *In arbitration,* arbitrators have only one case to decide at a time. They can give it their undivided attention and allow the parties as much time and as many hearings at different times as are needed. *In court,* in most jurisdictions after the case is called for trial, it continues until completed. There is no possibility of scheduling different hearings to accommodate busy and perhaps otherwise unavailable witnesses. Judges are always burdened by a large calendar of cases, a fact which may influence their patience. Judges are also often influenced by extraneous factors, such as favorable or unfavorable impression of, or past experience with, the legal counsel, or a natural tendency to identify one or both parties with the parties in other cases they have decided. In particular, it has been observed that the last case decided seems to have an influence upon the one that follows.
3. *In arbitration,* when a hearing is set, it will begin and be heard as scheduled. *In court,* the practice is to schedule more cases than can be

71

heard at a particular time. Otherwise, as a result of settlements and continuances the court may be left without anything to do while it still has a large calendar of waiting cases. This means that parties, witnesses, and attorneys must waste valuable time waiting for their case to be reached.

4. *In arbitration,* the hearing is private. Only the parties, their attorneys, witnesses, children, the arbitrator, and an FMA administrator may attend. *In court,* the general public may attend.

5. *In arbitration,* the few actually needed procedural guides are contained in the Marital Arbitration Rules which have been adopted by the parties. *In court,* procedure is determined by local court rules, statutory law, and rulings in hundreds of appellate court decisions. It is not surprising, then, that attorneys gain or lose advantages for their clients through procedural manipulations and that laymen are completely bewildered.

6. *In arbitration,* the arbitrator's decision is final. *In court,* an appeal or the threat of appeal with its attendant costs and delays may force concessions even when a just decision has been made. In practice, it is rare that parties will appeal what may actually be an unjust decision for the same reasons. Thus the right of appeal in most matrimonial cases is more a theoretical rather than a realizable advantage.

Other Characteristics

Under most state laws, arbitrators may require that testimony be given under oath with penalties for perjury. They may also compel the production of records and the attendance of witnesses, obtaining court orders if needed. However, since arbitration is always a voluntary process, it is rare that such powers are exercised, although it is not uncommon for witnesses to give testimony under oath. As in a court proceeding, a stenographic transcript may be made. Often the parties and the arbitrator will agree that an audiotape recording be made in place of a stenographic record at considerably less expense.

Parens Patriae

The doctrine of *parens patriae* means that the court, representing society, assumes a paternal concern aimed at ensuring that custody is appropriate and that adequate child support is provided. By contrast, in most other civil litigation, the parties are free to reach any settlement or agreement they wish, and the court will nearly always honor it. Exceptions to this are agreements which are illegal or are found by the court to be against public policy.

But marital litigation is a kind of civil litigation in which the parties are *not free* to make any agreement they wish. The parties' agreements with each other regarding custody and child support are subject to the court's approval, disapproval, or modification at any time as long as the children are minors.

Court Approval

The arbitrator's decision on matters relating to custody and child support must also receive the court's approval before it will be included in a judgment and decree. Typically, approval is made on the basis of a cursory examination of the agreement, with perhaps a question to whomever is presenting it. At a party's request, the court will reopen the issue for hearings when it believes that the arrangements for custody or support may not be in the best interests of the child.

Procedure

Mediation and arbitration are separate processes, operating under separate though compatible rules. It is therefore possible for a couple to seek arbitration of a controversy without having first reached impasse in mediation. Thus marital arbitration may become a useful resource for couples who have not used mediation. But mediation is a far better setting for decision making, since mutual decisions reached by the parties are much to be preferred over those made by an arbitrator.

The Marital Arbitration Rules specify the procedure to be followed by the parties. As a means of giving an overview of the process, a procedural sequence follows with the caution that, in the event of any seeming differences, the provisions of the rules will govern.

1. The parties reach an agreement to arbitrate. The Marital Mediation Rules include this agreement, so that no further agreement is required for couples who have been in mediation.
2. The specific issue to be decided by the arbitrator must be agreed upon. The mediator and the advisory attorney will assist the parties in clearly stating this issue or issues.
3. The agreement to arbitrate and the statement of the issue are filed with an FMA representative.
4. A cost deposit is made covering estimated amounts for FMA administration, arbitrator's services, and advisory attorney's fees.
5. FMA will submit to both parties, or their representatives, an identical

list of names from its panel of arbitrators. If the parties agree that arbitrators having certain training or experience are desired, FMA will make an effort to submit names of persons so qualified.

6. The parties will each cross out the names of any arbitrators who are unsatisfactory to them. The remaining names on the list will be numbered by each party in order of preference.

7. FMA will determine which arbitrators were given highest preference. It will then contact the arbitrators selected by the parties in order of preference and appoint the arbitrator having the highest preference who is willing to serve.

8. FMA will negotiate with the parties and the arbitrator so that the arbitrator can designate a time, date, and place for hearing which meets the convenience of all concerned as nearly as possible.

9. At the hearing, a representative of FMA will serve as a tribunal clerk for the purpose of overseeing FMA's responsibilities for providing administrative assistance to the arbitrator and the parties.

10. When the arbitrator has reached a decision (called an *award*), he or she will submit it to FMA for delivery to the parties.

11. In instances when the parties have reached a partial settlement in mediation, the advisory attorney selected by the parties will incorporate the arbitrator's award into the settlement agreement previously reached by the parties. But the preferred procedure is to redraft the entire agreement, incorporating the items previously agreed upon and the arbitrator's award into a single, complete agreement. When executed by the parties, this agreement becomes the final settlement agreement.

12. FMA then makes an accounting of the deposit or deposits paid by the parties, paying from it the arbitrator's and the administrator's fee and returning any remaining balance to the parties.

Suggested Readings

Marital Arbitration Rules, Appendix FMA-D.

9 Marital Mediators—Their Skills and Training

Background Required

A marital mediation service needs to have a panel of mediators with a varied background of training and life experience. Marriage and family counselors offer a knowledge of family dynamics, communications, and a desirable diversity of backgrounds. Psychotherapists and social workers, experienced in working with families, are well suited for training as mediators. Lawyers or others with legal experience have much to offer, but skills in behavioral science are usually lacking. It is generally easier for one trained in behavioral sciences to acquire legal and other knowledge required for mediation than for the legally trained person to gain knowledge and a feel for behavioral science and counseling skills.

Middle- and upper-income clients, such as those served by the presently developed Marital Mediation Rules, have fairly complex problems because of their high present and potential income, combined with substantial amounts of property. For these reasons, the background, training, and experience for marital mediators serving such clients must be considerably more extensive than will be required for serving clients with lower incomes.

Academic attainment seems to be a suitable means of indicating what is expected in the way of prerequisite education and equivalency, although FMA recognizes that not everyone meeting academic requirements may become an effective marital mediator. There are also those who lack academic credentials whose life experience has been such that they have the capacity for becoming successful mediators.

Nevertheless, a graduate-level degree in behavioral sciences or law, with the latter supplemented by substantial training in behavioral sciences, can be considered a basic requisite. Postacademic training and supervision should be comparable to that called for in states requiring licensing for marriage and family counselors, or the training required for clinical membership in the American Association of Marriage and Family Counselors. In general, these requirements are as follows:

Education: At least a master's degree in social work, psychology, psychological counseling, pastoral or marriage counseling, or the equivalent work experience as determined by FMA.

Experience: Three years of full-time counseling experience (or its equivalent as determined by FMA), two of which were in marriage and family counseling.

Special Skills Needed

While behavioral science training provides important skills needed by the marital mediator, a specific focus on interpersonal communication training is essential. Couples in mediation communicate with each other and with the mediator on many levels. Ulterior messages are heard or felt on a psychological level. Often a word, a facial expression, or a gesture can communicate an entire sequence of disruptive ulterior messages to the opposite party. The mediator who is well trained in interpersonal communication skills can recognize, confront, and reduce the incidence of these destructive messages. A simple example might be:

Mediator: I noticed he shrugged his shoulders when you said that. What did you feel he was saying to you?
Wife: What I say is not important.
Mediator (to husband): Were you aware of having shrugged your shoulders?
Husband: I guess I did.
Mediator: And what did you want to say right then, but didn't?
Husband: That she hadn't heard what I said just before she said that.
Mediator: So you each feel discounted when the other seems not to hear what you are saying. I can help you find ways of getting things straight with each other. Would you like that?
Husband and Wife: Yes.

Training in Transactional Analysis (TA) is one of the better ways of learning interpersonal communications skills. The mediator with sufficient TA training can follow a dialogue like the above example and analyze the transactions, consider possible interventions, and decide on the most appropriate timing for using them. Unlike with some other applications of TA, the mediator makes communications diagrams for himself mentally, but the couple is not aware of this process.

It is expected that a training curriculum and training materials will be developed for marital mediators. Different curricula will be offered for mediators working with clients at lower economic levels. Further research and evaluation of structured mediation in its present form and with variations in procedure are in planning stages as this book is written. It is an art that is evolving as experience in its use is gained.

Suggested Training

This book, supplemented by the suggested reading at the end of each chapter, makes it possible to begin a training program for marital mediators. The suggested reading found at the end of each chapter constitute an essential part of a mediator training program. They have been carefully selected with this purpose in mind and are not merely a general range of reference materials. The following is a proposed training sequence for marital mediators who have already acquired the education and the skills previously described in this chapter:

1. General overview of mediation and arbitration as applied in marital settlement (chapter 1)
2. Divorce and settlement when a marriage is dysfunctional (chapter 2)
3. The concept of structure, including a thorough study and explanation of the Marital Mediation Rules (chapter 3), as well as the rules and Orientation, parts I and II, in Appendixes FMA-A and FMA-B
4. Marital mediation and the legal profession (chapter 11)
5. The adversarial legal system; fault and no-fault divorce; divorce in the United States and other countries
6. Details of the divorce procedure in the state in which the mediator will practice
7. Training and practice in giving client orientation
8. The psychology of negotiating and bargaining; basic conflict resolution
9. Interpersonal communications training; Transactional Analysis; game analysis
10. Conducting the mediation session (chapter 4)
11. Theories and methods of mediation (chapter 10)
12. Postdivorce budgets for each party and children; double budget procedures in cases of controversy over custody (chapter 5)
13. The income statement for each party; gross income, take-home pay; contrasting income with cash flow
14. The statement of assets and liabilities (financial statement or balance sheet); methods of comparing financial statements prepared by the client for different purposes and at different times as a means of developing full disclosure of assets
15. Income tax returns, Form 1040; comparing returns with each other and with financial statements as a means of checking for full disclosure of assets
16. Examining corporate financial statements and profit and loss statements (operating statements); looking for concealed assets and income
17. Tax consequences of divorce (chapter 6)

18. The settlement agreement (chapter 7)
19. Arbitration of impasse (chapter 8)
20. Supervised role playing of mediation; peer critique followed by supervisor's critique
21. Observing mediation sessions, followed by critique from mediator
22. Conducting mediation under direct supervision, with each session followed by critique
23. Conducting mediation with tape supervision pending final certification by supervisor

Suggested Readings

See Bibliography for complete references.

Campos and McCormick, *Introduce Your Marriage to Transaction Analysis*.
Woolams, Brown, and Hugie, *Transactional Analysis in Brief*.
James and Jongeward, *Born to Win*.
Brown, "Divorce Counseling," in David H. L. Olsen, ed., *Treating Relationships*, p. 399.

10 Theories and Methods of Mediation

Marital mediation is an art in its early stages of development. The greater part of all research on conflict resolution has been carried out within the last ten years, and marital mediation is a pioneering application of that research. Demonstrated techniques for conflict resolution upon which a marital mediator can rely must await the outcome of future in-depth longitudinal research. However, we do know a great deal already about the subject, and this body of knowledge is one with which the mediator must be familiar.

Theoretical Foundations

To begin, there are the theoretical considerations from which rules in structured mediation have been developed. The resolution of conflict implies more than the mere cessation of conflict. Cessation of conflict may be mistaken for resolution in several instances, such as:

1. A party finds himself in a disadvantageous position and decides to withdraw, expecting to resume the controversy when conditions are more favorable.
2. One party is overwhelmed by the other's power. In extreme cases this may mean the death of the less powerful party.
3. A party passively accepts whatever terms the other party demands, but has no expectation of complying with them.

In none of these instances has resolution been reached. Achieving resolution of conflict requires that the following conditions be present:

1. The physical well-being of each party is maintained during negotiations and in the resolution reached.
2. The feelings of self-worth of each party are maintained during the negotiating process and in the resolution reached.
3. Each party respects or tolerates the opposite party as a person, while understanding that this does not imply approval of that party's morals or values.
4. All relevant facts, available options, and technical information are considered and used by the parties in reaching resolution.
5. The consequences of each available option are considered by both parties before a resolution is agreed upon.

6. The resolution reached is chosen by each party even though other choices were available.

These conditions suggest that a structure that fosters the resolution of conflict, rather than merely controlling or ending it, is a coherent integration of three separate structures: a procedural structure, a value structure, and a psychological structure. The *procedural structure* is basically intended to provide an orderly and expeditious process. It also plays a vital role in providing the means by which the parties can have available to them the factual and technical information required for making decisions. Additionally, it contributes significantly toward achieving a desirable psychological structure. While meeting these needs, the procedural structure must not be allowed to become so complex that the parties devote excessive energies to simply observing it or are encouraged to manipulate it to gain advantage.

The value structure must provide reasonably clear and rationally applicable criteria for resolving controversy. It is intended to establish basic ethical standards of fairness to be followed by the parties. While these standards must satisfy an elementary sense of fairness, they cannot be expected to satisfy the widely divergent ideas of what is just. Indeed, there are many things about life on this planet that are unfair, and the puny human efforts will not make it otherwise. Thus, it is more important that the value structure be understandable to the parties and fairly easily applicable by them, than that it meet every test of fairness.

The *psychological structure* must provide a setting in which the physical and emotional needs of the parties are sufficiently met that they can make maximum use of their rational abilities. The procedural structure contributes to this goal by limiting the issues considered in mediation, scheduling regular times for negotiations, establishing a neutral territory in which mediation is conducted, and giving the mediator the power to see that both parties follow the rules. The value structure also contributes by providing the parties with guidelines of fairness that are relatively specific and easy to follow.

The rules themselves do not establish any particular psychological structure. They are designed to create a context within which a well-trained mediator, using interpersonal communications skills, can maintain a psychological structure which will facilitate the resolution of conflict. A dysfunctional pattern of communications is nearly always present in couples who come for mediation; yet effective communications are essential. Thus constant and skillful monitoring of communications is one of the most important functions of the mediator.

Factors Affecting Cooperation

Beginning with the couple's first contact with the mediation process during the intake interview and orientation, efforts are made to motivate them to cooperate, to create what is called a *cooperative motivational orientation.*[1] There are three types of motivational orientations found in negotiating processes which may be defined as follows:

1. *Cooperative*—The person has a positive interest in the welfare of others as well as in his own welfare.
2. *Individualistic*—The person has an interest in doing as well as he can for himself and is unconcerned about the welfare of others.
3. *Competitive*—The person has an interest in doing better than others, as well as in doing as well as he can for himself.

Motivation

The rules in structured mediation are designed to create a context in which a *cooperative* motivational orientation can operate, since it is the only one of the three that results in resolution of conflicts. Let us look at some of the ways in which the mediator can get the parties to cooperate.

Sometimes the accomplishment of this objective is not so much a matter of what the parties do as what they do *not* do. A skilled mediator operating within the structure provided by the rules can deny to the parties those strategies that create competitive and individualistic motivational orientations. In addition, the mediator must use every means possible for establishing a spirit of cooperation between the parties. Each mediator will eventually develop his own techniques. However, two general suggestions may be made.

First, observe the parties carefully, looking for any indications of cooperative behavior. Call attention to them and compliment the party for such behavior. If one party offers cooperation and the other seems not to notice, quickly call the party's attention to the offer of cooperation in such a way as to encourage similar behavior. Second, look for opportunities to assign small tasks which require the parties' cooperation. Be sure that both parties are willing to perform the tasks, and abandon the project if there is indication that hostilities will develop. An example of a mutually cooperative task would be asking the husband to help the wife figure out that part of her budget relating to automotive repairs, expenses, insurance, and the like. The wife may then reciprocate by helping the husband work out that part of his budget which relates to food, clothing, laundry, and so forth. If the mediator feels it is unwise for the couple to do this at home, it may be done during the session.

Another significant factor influencing motivational orientations in mediation is the extent to which either a competitive or an individualistic orientation is already operating between the parties. During a period of one to three weeks following physical separation, most couples are not yet displaying signs of escalation of their antagonistic feelings toward each other. This, then, is a critical time, because the process of escalation will overtake most of them before they are fully aware of what is happening.

If the couple comes into mediation before escalation has begun, there is a good likelihood that they will establish a cooperative motivational orientation. Unfortunately, too many couples believe they can work things out for themselves without the controls provided by a mediator, and they delay coming into mediation until after their feelings have escalated to a high degree of competitive and individualistic orientation. When this happens, it is considerably more difficult to establish a cooperative atmosphere.

From this it can be seen that another principle is involved—that it is considerably easier to move from a cooperative motivational orientation to either a competitive or individualistic one, than from either or both of these to a cooperative one. An examination of this phenomenon may be found in Deutsch's studies of trust and suspicion in which it has been observed that it is easier to move from trust (when it is violated) to suspicion than to move from suspicion (when it is negated) to trust.[1]

Basic Psychological Needs

In order to move husband and wife toward a rational resolution of their conflicts, mediators must also be aware of some of the basic psychological needs which are present in both parties in varying proportions, depending on the situation. They are the need for achievement, the need for affiliation, and the need for power. The *need for achievement* may be defined as the need or desire to attain a standard of excellence. The *need for affiliation* (or nurturance) is the need or desire to have friendly relations with others. And the *need for power* (or dominance) is the need or desire to exert control over others. During the mediation sessions, the mediator can use observation and intuition for estimating which of these three basic psychological motivations appears to be most active in each of the parties. The mediator's assessment made in this way can suggest interventions that may motivate the parties toward cooperation and settlement.

In any case, conflicts resulting from these three basic needs are challenges to the mediator's intervention skills. Since the mediator is not likely to bring about a change in both parties simultaneously, the best procedure is to work first with the party who is most likely to be responsive. If interventions with that party are successful, interventions with the other party may become possible since that party will now need to change his or her responses to reflect the changes made by the first party.

Using Transactional Analysis

Mediators need not be trained in the full range of Transactional Analysis theory and practice, but it is essential that they have a thorough understanding of ego states and have the ability to diagnose them from moment to moment as transactions take place between husband and wife. Mediators must also understand the rules of communication and game analysis. With this training, they will have techniques available for redirecting communications when they become counterproductive.

However, sometimes the changes in direction of communications are so rapid and confusing that it is impossible to follow the machinations of the parties, and efforts to do so can cause even a third party to feel disoriented. In these cases, the mediator must intervene decisively and simply stop the conflict. If it is not stopped, it can easily lead to violence, either physical or psychological. At an early stage in the mediation process, mediators may ask both parties for permission to ask them to stop talking at times. Here is the time to use that permission.

Once the conflict has been stopped, both parties will be feeling agitated and disoriented, as might be expected. While admonishing one party to remain silent, the mediator may begin by asking the other party to get in touch with his or her feelings. If this leads to further blaming or accusations of the opposite party, the mediator must stop this and ask the party again to just talk about his or her own feelings. When the party finally does express these feelings, it can provide a catharsis which may open the way for more rational negotiations. The process should then be repeated with the second party. Finally, the mediator should ask both parties what they feel after having heard what the other party was feeling.

Fortunately, people do have a rational conflict style which is characterized by a cooperative motivational orientation. The mediator's role in this case is to compliment the parties and encourage them to continue. Decisions reached in this style of conflict will be supported by both parties, and both will experience respect for self and the opposite party.

Dealing with Problems of Reorganization

The overall problem to be resolved in mediation is how the needs of each family member can be met within the limits fixed by available resources. Resources may be thought of as consisting of material accumulations, marketable skills each person possesses, and the potential for further development of skills. Another major problem is the rearrangement of parenting relationships, and there are considerably more social constraints involved in dealing with parenting than with resources. For example, if the father is given custody of the children, even by agreement, the mother will be subject to criticism by friends and family. "How could you give up your children?" she will be asked.

Because arrangements regarding parenting also influence allocation of resources, it is often difficult to tell in which area the controversy is really focused. A woman may realize that she can make a better case asking for child support than for alimony, and a man may be more willing to make payments labeled child support. But this willingness may vanish when he realizes that the woman can spend his payments in any way she chooses, no matter how they are labeled. When the woman gets custody of the children, she has two possible claims through which she may receive support from her former spouse. Without custody, her only claim is for alimony, which has considerably less appeal. Men have not overlooked this point and may be motivated to contest custody support for strategic reasons. It is in this way that children can become pawns in a financial struggle.

The rationale followed in marital mediation is to have the couple focus on allocation of resources and defer any controversies relating to parenting until after these issues are resolved. While there are insufficient data to generalize from our experience to date, it appears that controversies over custody and parenting have been reduced by following this procedure.

Suggested Readings

See Bibliography for complete references.

Rubin and Brown, *The Social Psychology of Bargaining and Negotiation.*
Deutsch, *The Resolution of Conflict.*

Notes

1. Motivational orientations are described in detail in Morton Deutsch, *The Resolution of Conflict.*

11 Marital Mediation and the Legal Profession

The Attorney's Role

General Concepts

Marital mediation has been designed to serve couples needing legal and other skilled guidance. Its process focuses the services of the attorney on those areas which require the exercise of legal *judgment*. Therefore the attorney is *not* required to use time to conduct negotiations leading up to the point where the exercise of legal judgment is needed. These negotiations can be conducted less expensively and usually more effectively by a marital mediator who is specially equipped and trained to handle problems involving interpersonal conflict resolution. Lawyers are not as well equipped to provide these services, because of their lack of training in the behavioral sciences, as well as the ethical restrictions under which they must practice. This does not mean that the marital mediator is less ethical than the attorney. The difference lies in their roles.

The invariable role of the marital mediator is that of a neutral third party, while the usual role of the attorney is that of an advocate for one party. An attorney who represents one party as an advocate cannot ethically give advice to the opposite party. Attorneys have sometimes undertaken, on an informal basis, to assume a neutral posture with clients. Because they were, or eventually became, an advocate for one party, they have found themselves facing charges before a disciplinary board, or have become the defendant in a malpractice action, or both. The reasons for this are clear. Successful conduct of a neutral process requires substantial external structure within which the parties, the attorneys, and the mediators operate. The Marital Mediation Rules provide such a structure. The practice of law does not.

Establishing a Center

The operation of any marital mediation service requires an overview of professionals trained in law and the behavioral sciences. In recent years, more lawyers have begun to seek training in the behavioral sciences as a complement to their legal training, but those with substantial training and experience in the behavioral sciences are still a rare breed.

The attorney's role with respect to a marital mediation service not only involves the overview of client services, but also requires continuous liason with the legal profession. Unless the attorney is already thoroughly familiar with the Code of Professional Responsibility (Canons of Ethics) in his or her state, a thorough and careful study is indicated before the first contact is made with fellow attorneys and the bar association announcing that a marital mediation service is about to be established.

At this first contact with the bar association, it is highly desirable that attorneys bring with them a carefully drafted written statement, accompanied by supporting documents, outlining in detail the operational policies and procedures which will be followed by the mediation service. It is helpful if this statement includes specific references to the Code of Professional Responsibility, supporting each step in the procedure as it is described. An example of such a statement (Report of Legal Service Plan) can be found in Appendix FMA-G.

Each state bar association establishes its own code of professional responsibility based upon those developed by the American Bar Association. But each state makes its own variations and often establishes standards in addition to the canons, directory rules, and ethical considerations found in the ABA version. For the sake of uniform reference here, the current (August 1976) ABA code has been used. A copy may be obtained from the ABA, a local bar association, or volume 6 of the *Martindale-Hubbell Law Directory*.

The present code makes it necessary that marital mediation services in which lawyers participate be conducted only through a nonprofit community organization (DR2-102D). While not specifically called for by the Code, it is recommended that any such organization support its position by obtaining certification from the Internal Revenue Service that it is a nonprofit organization, donations to which are deductible against income. Such a certification places the organization within the scope of nonprofit organizations which enjoy exemptions contemplated by the Code of Professional Responsibility. Other types of nonprofit organizations, of which there are many, may or may not qualify. A mediation service may be operated by a nonprofit corporation organized for that purpose.

The recently decided Bates case may open the door for lawyer participation, under FMA rules, for proprietary agencies. (In *Arizona Bar v. Bates*, the U.S. Supreme Court on June 27, 1977 found in favor of Bates, thus allowing advertising in the legal profession.) With FMA certification, such an agency would become a mediation center. Lawyer and mediator participation would be through FMA panel membership. Nonpanel lawyers (but not mediators) may also be used by such a center. Certification of a center by FMA or an authorized training institution also provides the advantages of having supervision and consultation in connection with the many problems related to service delivery, as well as with relationships between the community and legal profession.

Attorneys' Objections

When any new marital mediation service is established in a community, it will surely be seen as a threat by some members of the legal profession. Such attorneys may have no interest in learning about how the service operates or what its policies are. They simply want it to go away and may expend substantial energies looking for some means of bringing about its departure from the scene.

Defensive Tactics

One attorney asserted in a number of public appearances that he knew of a client who had gotten wrong legal advice through "a local service." Even though FMA was not named, it was sufficiently well known in the community for the reference to be clear. When confronted, the attorney acknowledged that it was not FMA that had given legal advice but rather one of its panel attorneys. Further investigation demonstrated that the attorney had not given incorrect legal advice.

Even if the charge had been true, giving incorrect legal advice (especially in the opinion of other lawyers) is certainly far from unknown in the legal profession. Besides, the Code of Professional Responsibility (DR2-101D) prohibits FMA from interfering in any manner with the impartial advisory attorney's legal advice. It is the attorney's professional responsibility to give such advice, not that of FMA.

Criticisms

The following is a sampling, from FMA experience, of the kinds of criticisms which may be directed toward a mediation center by lawyers, along with some suggestions on how to respond when necessary.

"FMA is engaging in the unauthorized practice of law." Neither FMA nor the mediator is engaging in the practice of law. The licensed advisory attorney is doing so. The fact that lawyers, on occasion, serve as mediators or perform mediation functions does not make mediation the practice of law. If it did, the Mediation and Conciliation Service of the United States Department of Labor, as well as numerous labor mediators who are not lawyers, are engaging in the unauthorized practice of law.

"People who are not lawyers are giving legal advice." This suggests that either FMA or the mediators are giving legal advice. As has been indicated earlier, the bare mention of a provision of law or a statute by a mediator or other staff person does not in itself constitute legal advice or the practice of law. The exercise of legal judgment as to *how* the statute or other provision applies to the client's situation is the practice of law (see EC 3-5).

Mediators do hear attorneys advising clients over and over about the same legal issues and thus become fairly familiar with laws relating to divorce settlements. Indeed such familiarity with legal principles is part of the marital mediator's training. It is useful to the mediator in providing general guidance during mediation, with a clear understanding that all matters requiring the exercise of legal judgment are solely the responsibility of the advisory attorney. Any preliminary directions taken at the suggestion of the mediator are subject to final approval by an attorney before either party is allowed to act upon or be bound by them.

"The parties were not given full, complete legal advice." In some sense, this is true. Parties require only legal advice which is appropriate to their situation. What is appropriate is a matter of legal judgment, and it is not uncommon for lawyers to disagree over such matters. Considering the standards of thoroughness established by FMA for panel attorneys who draft settlement agreements, it is hardly likely that clients will receive less adequate legal advice than is the common experience of legal consumers.

"The Code of Professional Responsibility forbids lawyers to associate themselves with nonlawyers." This is correct (DR3-103-A). This is why a lawyer and, say, a marriage and family counselor could not provide joint services. Moreover, attorneys who are also licensed marriage and family counselors are forbidden to indicate this fact on their letterheads, in a professional publication relating to marriage counseling, or even on their office doors (see DR2-102E). However, the Code of Professional Responsibility does allow a lawyer to associate himself with a nonprofit community organization which provides legal service as a portion of its overall services to clients or beneficiaries (see DR2-103D).

"If the mediation service advertises, then lawyers who are associated with it benefit by that advertising and are themselves engaged in improper solicitation." This extreme proscription against advertising is no longer valid since the United States Supreme Court decided the Bates case. In addition, the present Code of Professional Responsibility does allow a qualified legal assistance organization to advertise its services, and lawyers associating themselves with it are not in violation of the code (see EC 2-15).

"The impartial advisory attorney cannot advise both parties without violating the conflict-of-interest provisions of the Code of Professional Responsibility." That provision refers to a situation in which an attorney must represent one party as an advocate. In such a situation, an attorney

may not give legal advice to the opposite party. It has been said that a lawyer represents conflicting interests, when, in behalf of one client, it is his/her duty to contend for that which duty to another client requires him/her to oppose. Under the Marital Mediation Rules, however, impartial advisory attorneys are not advocates for either party. They are mandated by the rules to give fair, equal, and impartial advice to both parties. This role for attorneys with respect to parties having a conflict of interest is provided for and sanctioned by the Code of Professional Responsibility (see DR5-105C, EC 5-14, EC 5-15, and EC 5-16).

"Bias was exercised in the selection of the panel of impartial advisory attorneys." Bias is a popular charge often hurled at a screening process one does not like. Any mediation service that selects its panel attorneys on a biased basis is not likely to operate very long. But a mediation service does have every right to screen advisory attorneys on the basis of character, experience, and competence. Further, when it becomes evident from an attorney's performance that poor judgment was exercised in admitting that attorney to the panel, his or her name should be removed.

"Some panel attorneys are not properly qualified to serve as legal advisors in marital controversies." As has just been pointed out, FMA must look very carefully at the qualifications of its panel attorneys with the help of its liaison attorney. But just as lawyers differ in matters of legal judgment, they also differ in their opinions of one another. No lawyer will be considered well qualified in the eyes of *all* his/her colleagues.

"The mediation service is providing legal referral in competition with the bar association's referral service." Perhaps this is so. Legal referral is a separate service. If the mediation service as a nonprofit organization chooses to provide this additional service, it may do so under the recently revised Code of Professional Responsibility (EC 2-15). It must be noted that the Code does call for advance notification to the state disciplinary board whenever a legal service is to be provided through a nonprofit organization [DR2-101D(4)G]. Marital mediation under FMA's rules is considered a legal service under this provision.

"The mediation service is interfering with the lawyer and his/her client when, during an ongoing controversy, the parties decide to mediate their differences." At times lawyers forget that they are in the employ of their clients, who have the clear right to determine how they will be represented and to terminate the attorney's employment if they so decide. Other lawyers refuse to represent a client who does not give them virtually unlimited discretion in handling the case. Whenever mediation is decided upon the parties and they are already represented by attorneys, the mediation service must insist that the parties notify the attorneys of their decision. It is good practice for the service to check directly with the attorney to be sure that this notification has been received.

"I would never allow my client to mediate because she might have to pay her husband alimony." It is true that this could happen under the provisions of the Marital Mediation Rules. If the Equal Rights Amendment is adopted, it will also be possible under the law of every state in the union. (As of 1978 only thirteen states make no provision for the husband to receive alimony, and constitutional questions have been raised in these states.) On the other hand, in our experience to date, no wife has been required to pay her husband alimony. A common gambit of attorneys is to focus on the remote and unlikely event because, for lack of precedent, there is no basis to argue convincingly under what circumstances it might happen and what the outcome might be if it did. And, as every lawyer knows, it is always easier to make assertions than to refute them. Furthermore, it takes attention away from more pertinent issues.

"Guidelines for property settlement, spousal maintenance, and child support are not the same as state law." This is correct. State laws are often vague homilies lacking in specifics, so that the court has virtually unbridled discretion to decide these issues as it sees fit. This accounts for the wide discrepancies in outcome found among judges who are serving under the same law. For example, Chapter 40 of the Illinois Revised Statutes provides:

When a divorce is decreed, the court may make such order touching the alimony and maintenance of the wife or husband, the care, custody, and support of the children, or any of them, from the circumstances of the parties and the nature of the case, including default cases: the court shall make inquiry with respect to the children of the parties, if any, and shall make such order touching the care, custody, support, and education of the minor children of the parties or any of them, as shall be deemed proper and for the benefit of the children.

The state of Illinois has not been singled out as a bad example. Indeed, its laws are very consistent with those of most other states. It was selected because this particular provision of law and the functioning of the judiciary under it have been the subject of an in-depth study entitled "The Divorce Process: Views of the Illinois Judiciary."[1] Using the above statute as a springboard, each judge who responded tended to follow his/her own set of criteria which at times differed substantially from that adopted by other judges in the study. With such poor statutory guidelines, there is little wonder that there is inconsistency in court findings and that parties are not able to judge whether they were treated fairly.

"I would never want my client to mediate because the rules call for arbitration, and I don't believe in arbitration." Our only comment is that attorneys perhaps have had unpleasant experiences with arbitration. Such experiences are usually in arbitrations that are not conducted under rules of procedure, such as the Marital Arbitration Rules or the rules of the

American Arbitration Association. Doubtless the same attorney has also had unpleasant results in the courts, but since this is a more familiar setting, these experiences are more easily accepted and forgotten. Again, this is another instance in which the attorney is focusing on the remote and unlikely. To date, less than 1 percent of couples in mediation have found it necessary to resort to arbitration.

"What is there for the lawyer to do when mediation is completed?" Here is the crux of the matter, and the answer is, "Not much." With a well-drafted, signed settlement agreement in hand, some mediation clients may decide to handle their own divorces. This has not been FMA's experience to date, but it is likely that some members of the legal profession are not far off target when they predict that this will happen. Even if the divorce is handled by an attorney, it is a ministerial ritual for which only a very nominal fee can be charged.

The Do-It-Yourself Movement

There is, of course, growing evidence that lawyers' fears are well grounded, as the increasing number of do-it-yourself divorces following the adoption of no-fault laws in recent years has demonstrated. The public demand for no-fault divorce legislation, which began in the early 1970s, is not likely to be turned back by the legal profession. That the economic implications of no-fault divorce are a concern of the legal profession is clear, and marital mediation can be expected to heighten these concerns. Charles Mentrowski, associate dean of Marquette Law School, chided the members of the Family Law Section about this:

I really relish this no-fault business that you lawyers talk about. Behind it all, can't you see that it's really no-lawyer? Whether it is no-fault insurance law or administrative probate or now no-fault divorce, you're all advocating your own demise. The reformers have done such a fine job, they've made themselves no longer necessary. Of course, I can talk this way because I don't rely on the practice of law for my income.[2]

The contention of the legal profession that the public is suffering widespread injury and damage as a result of using do-it-yourself divorce kits or in other ways obtaining *pro se* divorces is not supported, according to a study made at Yale University Law School. The authors state:

Although the organized Bar has always contended that its unauthorized practice campaign is not a "trade union movement," but a service "in the public interest," none of its suits against divorce concerns has developed a record of more than minimal mishaps attributable to lay assistance. And none of the judicial opinions in those cases challenge the accuracy of the published or verbal instructions at issue. Indeed, one court explicitly held that even a perfect record of consumer satisfaction would be "irrelevant."[3]

With few exceptions, persons who obtained their own divorces using kits or other means have been well satisfied with the results. One author of a California do-it-yourself divorce kit has estimated that users of the kit have saved themselves over $50 million in legal fees.[4] A part of the Cavanaugh and Rhode research demonstrated that an average attorney's fee for an uncontested divorce is $500 and that clients were much less satisfied with the results. Their attorneys acknowledged having spent an average of four hours of time per case, and the settlement agreement was substantially worked out by the couple in advance of contacting the attorney. In addition, 79 percent of clients reported they received no tax advice, even though attorneys asserted that this was an important part of their service.

The foregoing discussion must not be taken as a general recommendation that divorcing couples should use do-it-yourself divorce kits or that they should attempt to obtain their own divorces by other means. At present the published do-it-yourself kits and lay services vary widely in cost and quality, and one is not necessarily indicative of the other. If a couple has no children, their marriage has been of short duration, and such marital property as they possess has been divided, all they may need, as one couple put it, is an eraser. This couple, given guidance through a well-designed kit or from other lay sources, can most likely succeed in obtaining a divorce at minimal cost and risk. Such a couple may not need an attorney and may not need mediation either.

Suggested Readings

See Bibliography for complete references.

Cavanaugh and Rhode, "The Unauthorized Practice of Law and Pro Se Divorce."
Coogler, "Changing the Lawyer's Role in Matrimonial Practice."
Eisler, *Dissolution.*

Notes

1. Walter D. Johnson, "The Divorce Process: Views of the Illinois Judiciary," Research paper, Department of Economics and Legislative Studies, Sangamon State University, Springfield, Illinois, 1976.
2. Wheeler, *No-Fault Divorce*, p. 120.
3. Cavanaugh and Rhode, "The Unauthorized Practice of Law and Pro Se Divorce," p. 113, 114.
4. *Crossing the Bar*, Wall Street Journal, September 3, 1976, p. 1.

Selected Bibliography

Books and Pamphlets

Atkin, Edith, and Rubin, Estelle. *Part Time Father*. New York: Vanguard Press, 1976.

Auerbach, Sylvia. *Your Money—How to Make It Stretch*. New York: Doubleday, 1974.

Bass, Howard L., and Rein, M.L. *Divorce or Marriage—A Legal Guide*. Englewood Cliffs, N.J.: Prentice-Hall, 1976.

Bernard, Jessie. *The Future of Marriage*. New York: World Publishing, 1972.

_____ . *The Future of Motherhood*. New York: The Dial Press, 1974.

Blodgett, Richard E. *The New York Times Book of Money*. New York: Quadrangle, 1971.

Bohannan, Paul, ed. *Divorce and After*. Garden City, N.Y.: Doubleday, 1971.

Campos, Leonard, and McCormick, Paul. *Introduce Your Marriage to Transactional Analysis*. San Joaquin TA Institute, 2732 Pacific Avenue, Stockton, CA 95204, 1972.

Caplow, Theodore. *Two Against One*. Englewood Cliffs, N.J.: Prentice-Hall, 1968.

Despert, J. Louise. *Children of Divorce*. Garden City, N.Y.: Dolphin, 1962.

Deutsch, Morton. *The Resolution of Conflict*. New Haven, Conn.: Yale University Press, 1973.

DeWolf, Rose. *Bonds of Acrimony*. Philadelphia: J.B. Lippincott, 1970.

Eisler, Riane Tennenhaus. *Dissolution*. New York: McGraw-Hill, 1977.

Epstein, Joseph. *Divorced in America: Marriage in an Age of Possibility*. New York: E.P. Dutton, 1974.

Gardner, Richard A. *The Boy's and Girl's Book about Divorce*. New York: Bantam Books, 1971.

Gettleman, Susan, and Markowitz, Janet. *The Courage to Divorce*. New York: Simon & Schuster, 1974.

Goldstein, Joseph; Freud, Anna; and Solnit, Albert J. *Beyond the Best Interests of the Child*. New York: Free Press Division of McMillan, 1973.

Goode, William J. *Women in Divorce*. New York: The Free Press, 1956.

Grunebaum, Henry, and Christ, Jacob, eds. *Contemporary Marriage: Structure, Dynamics, and Therapy*. Boston: Little, Brown, 1976.

Hunt, Morton, and Hunt, Bernice. *The Divorce Experience*. New York: McGraw-Hill, 1977.

Hurley, Glae E. *Personal Money Management—A Consumer Guide.* Englewood Cliffs, N.J.: Prentice-Hall, 1976.

James, Muriel, and Jongeward, Dorothy, *Born to Win.* Reading, Mass.: Addison-Wesley, 1971.

Janis, Irving L., and Mann, Leon. *Decision Making.* New York: The Free Press, 1977.

Kessler, Sheila. *The American Way of Divorce: Prescription for Change.* Chicago: Nelson-Hall, 1975.

Lasser, J.K., Institute. *Managing Your Famiy Finances.* New York: Doubleday, 1968.

Lindley, Alexander. *Separation Agreements and Ante-Nuptial Contracts.* New York: Matthew Bender, 1976.

Moffet, Robert R., and Scherer, Jack F. *Dealing with Divorce.* Boston: Little, Brown, 1976.

National Council on Family Relations. *Divorce and Divorce Reform: Task Force Report,* Emily M. Brown, Chairperson, 1219 University Avenue Southeast, Minneapolis, 1974.

O'Gorman, H.J. *Lawyers and Matrimonial Causes: A Study of Informal Pressures in Private Professional Practice.* New York: The Free Press, 1963.

Olson, David H.L., ed. *Treating Relationships.* Lake Mills, Iowa: Graphic Publishing Co., 1976.

O'Neil, William. *Divorce in the Progressive Era.* New Haven, Conn.: Yale University Press, 1967.

Rheinstein, Max. *Marriage Stability, Divorce, and the Law.* Chicago: University of Chicago Press, 1972.

Richards, Arlene, and Willis, Irene. *How to Get It Together When Your Parents Are Coming Apart.* New York: David MacKay, 1976.

Rubin, Jeffrey A., and Brown, Bert R. *The Social Psychology of Bargaining and Negotiation.* New York: Academic Press, 1975.

Sherman, Charles E. *How to Do Your Own Divorce in California.* Occidental, Calif.: Nolo Press, 1972.

Stotter, Lawrence H. *Drafting the Marital Settlement Agreement: Strategies and Techniques.* New York: Practicing Law Institute, 1977.

U.S. Department of Agriculture. *A Guide to Budgeting for the Family,* Home and Garden Bulletin No. 108. Rev. March 1976. Washington: Government Printing Office, 1976.

————. *Family Economics Review.* Consumer and Food Economics Institute, Agricultural Research Service, ARS-NE-36, Hyattsville, Md. 20782.

U.S. Department of Labor. *The Consumer Price Index.* Bureau of Labor Statistics. Washington: Government Printing Office, 1971.

_____ . *A Guide to Living Costs.* Atlanta, Ga.: Bureau of Labor Statistics, 1976.

_____ . *Three Standards of Living for an Urban Family of Four Persons,* Bureau of Labor Statistics Bulletin 1570-5. National Technical Information Service, U.S. Department of Commerce, Spring 1967.

Watts, Alan W. *The Wisdom of Insecurity.* New York: Vintage Books, 1951.

Weiss, Robert S. *Marital Separation.* New York: Basic Books, 1975.

Wheeler, Michael. *No-Fault Divorce.* Boston: Beacon Press, 1974.

Women in Transition, Inc. *Women in Transition: A Feminist Handbook on Separation and Divorce.* New York: Scribner's, 1975.

Woolams, Stanley; Brown, Michael; and Hugie, Kristyn. *Transactional Analysis in Brief.* Huron Valley Institute, 6869 Marshall Rd., Dexter, Mich. 48130, 1974.

Journals

Bernstein, Barton E. "Lawyer and Counselor as an Interdisciplinary Team: Preparing the Father for Custody." *Journal of Marriage and Family Counseling* 3 (July 1977):3.

Cavanaugh, Ralph C., and Rhode, Deborah L. "The Unauthorized Practice of Law and Pro Se Divorce." *Yale Law Journal* 86 (November 1976):1.

Coogler, O.J. "Changing the Lawyer's Role in Matrimonial Practice." *The Conciliation Courts Review* 15 (September 1977):1

The National Council on Family Relations. Special Issue: "The Family and the Law." *The Family Coordinator* 26 (October 1977):4.

Roman Melvin. "The Disposable Parent." *The Conciliation Courts Review* 15 (December 1977):2.

Films

Kessler, Sheila, and Whitley, John. "Divorce: Part I and Part II." Washington: American Personnel and Guidance Association, 1975.

List of Appendixes

Appendix FMA-A
Orientation, Part I
An Overview of Marital Mediation and the Legal System

Couples come to a marital mediation center for one of the following reasons:

1. Something about their marriage is not working, and they are considering the possibility of either divorce or separation. At this point what the couple needs is information about what is involved in case they decide to either separate or both separate and seek a divorce. They may also wish to explore with a third party their reasons for considering divorce.

2. The couple has not decided whether to seek a divorce, but has decided to live separately for some period of time after which they might then either resume their marital relationship or obtain a divorce.

3. The couple has already separated or plans to do so in the near future, and either one party or both parties have finally decided to seek a divorce.

4. The couple is already divorced, and the provisions made in the divorce decree regarding support or visitation or custody are not working. This may be because of changed financial circumstances or other changed life situations. Another reason may be that the divorce settlement itself is vague in certain areas, so that the parties are not able to agree upon its meaning.

Mediation under the Marital Mediation Rules is a means of developing workable arrangements for the couple and their children in the last three situations described. Some centers may offer a range of services aimed at helping couples in the first situation.

Couples coming to mediation are usually experiencing anxiety and stress which cover other feelings including anger, resentment, rejection, disappointment, helplessness, and a sense of loss. The need most commonly associated with these feelings is for support, often expressed as "wanting somebody on my side." The greater one's feelings of helplessness, the more one feels one must have a very strong ally on his or her side.

It is not surprising, then, that lawyers are often perceived as the logical choice for fulfilling this need, and lawyers themselves support this notion. When a party decides to fulfill the need for support by employing an attorney advocate, there is usually little or no awareness of how this may become the first move in an escalating competitive struggle between the parties that can become devastating both financially and emotionally. It is also a process in which each party denies his/her role in the destructive escalation, contending that the opposite party or the opposite attorney was responsible. Attorneys, too, despite their familiarity with the process, almost invariably deny their own responsibility, externalizing it upon the other side of the controversy.

Most couples do wish to avoid a destructive, competitive struggle, but there is much cultural support for the idea that in such situations one party will win and the other will lose. Thus each party becomes committed to "winning" in the belief that he/she is destined to be either a "winner" or a "loser." The same idea suggests that whatever one party receives is his or her gain and the other party's loss. The importance of maintaining a cooperative working relationship, even when there are children, is forgotten. Competitively reached settlement agreements have an extremely poor record for performance.

Marital mediation offers a quite different approach to resolving conflicts between the parties. It asserts that, even though the parties have decided that they can no longer continue living together as husband and wife, they believe:

1. I am entitled to full respect as a person.
2. The opposite party is entitled to the same respect.
3. Neither party has an investment in "winning" over the other in terms of money, property, or other conditions of the settlement.
4. Each party is interested in surviving through having his or her own needs met to the extent permitted by available resources, and each is equally interested in seeing that the opposite party's needs are also met. Both parties know that any settlement not meeting these conditions will not last.
5. Difficult as it may be to acknowledge, there is still caring between the parties, even though it may not be of the kind that would support a marital relationship. It is especially important that both parties acknowledge this fact when they will continue to provide parenting for their children, even though they will no longer be married to each other.

Parties considering mediation as a means of reaching settlement are understandably fearful that they will not receive the support they need. Further, it is realistically true that each party, and perhaps one more than the other, is confronted with making decisions about financial matters in which he or she has had little or no previous experience. Typically both parties will have given little consideration to matters of family finance or budgeting. Neither a lawyer nor a mediator can tell a party what his or her needs are, nor will either prepare a budget for that person. This is the responsibility of the party, both in mediation as well as in the adversarial legal system.

When one party perceives the other as more powerful, how can the less powerful party keep from being overwhelmed? Parties are not overwhelmed because mediation:

1. Teaches the parties how to be responsible for themselves now, so that they may be better able to cope with their life situation after divorce.
2. Spends more hours in working out a settlement than is typical in the adversarial legal process. Neither party is pressured into making a premature decision or making a decision without having had full opportunity to consider all relevant facts.
3. Supports cooperative rather than competitive processes for reaching a decision.
4. Uses the Marital Mediation Rules which ensure each party a setting in which he or she will have full opportunity to be heard. The opposite party will not be allowed to employ tactics which prevent this.

The most valuable part of the mediation process is in its insistence that each party take responsibility for his own life. As they respond to this, parties frequently come to appreciate their own strength in ways they had not previously experienced. In this, as in nearly all life situations, each individual is responsible for his own life. He is inviting disappointment when he expects others to take over that responsibility. Even if some of a person's responsibility is taken over by an attorney, for example, there will be an abrupt loss of the dependent relationship with the attorney once the divorce has been concluded.

It is important that both parties recognize that nearly all divorces result in both parties having a reduction in life-style. Typically the resources which were barely sufficient to support one household must now somehow be divided between two. It is understandable, then, that if one party wants the divorce more than the other, the party who least wants the divorce is likely to feel cheated. The parties may be able to work through their feelings around this issue, but no process, neither mediation nor any other, can be relied upon to avoid such feeling.

When a marriage is not working to the point that the parties begin to consider divorce, the divorce itself tends to be a threshold through which they believe they must pass as a precondition for everything else. Most parties, for example, believe that a divorce cannot be obtained without the consent of both parties. This leads to the mistaken idea that withholding agreement to divorce can be used for financial leverage. Rational as it might be to allow parties to obtain a divorce on the basis of mutual consent, the law takes quite an opposite position. Not only is mutual consent not required, but until the advent of no-fault divorce (now found in some fifteen states) the law specifically prohibited any agreement by the parties to obtain a divorce. Such agreements are considered contrary to "public policy" and are thus void. Moreover, even a settlement agreement which is based upon mutual agreement to obtain a divorce is void. On the other hand, the possibility of one party's preventing the other party from obtaining a divorce is rare indeed, and impossible in most states. If such a tactic should succeed in one state, there is nothing which would prevent the party from going to another state and obtaining a divorce there.

Once the parties accept the fact that divorce itself is not the issue, then they are in a better position to consider the four issues which must be resolved:

1. Division of marital property
2. Spousal maintenance for the dependent spouse
3. Child support, when there are dependent children
4. Custody and visitation arrangements

After thinking about the above issues, the next question most parties ask is, "What are my legal rights?"

Most parties believe that the law provides an answer to this question and for that reason hasten to find an attorney who will furnish it. The law does not specifically answer this question, as is commonly supposed. Consequently, the attorney's answer cannot be more specific than the law itself. The attorney offers opinions, but the attorney's opinions and what the law actually provides are difficult for the layman to separate. However accurate the attorney's opinions may be, they are predicated upon facts presented through the perceptions of the client. The attorney's opinion may change once these same facts are presented through the perceptions of the opposite party.

One may then ask, "If the law does not tell me what my rights are, then what does it say?" This question is best answered by providing an example which is typical of the laws of most states.

Chapter 40 of the *Illinois Revised Statutes* provides:

When a divorce is decreed, the court may make such order touching the alimony and maintenance of the wife or husband, the care, custody, and support of the children, or any of them, from the circumstances of the parties and the nature of the case, as shall be fit, reasonable, and just, and in all cases, including default cases, the court shall make inquiry with respect to the children of the parties, if any, and shall make such order touching the care, custody, support, and education of the minor children of the parties or any of them, as shall be deemed proper and for the benefit of the children.

With only such homilies as a guide, judges can and do decide upon the legal rights of the parties from a position of virtually unbridled discretion. An Illinois statute was selected for this example because it was part of a study conducted at Sangamon State University. The study found that Illinois judges' decisions under this statute showed little consistency among judges making decisions under this law. Similar inconsistencies were also found among cases where apparently the same factual situation was considered by a single judge.

If the law does not say what a party's rights are, how can mediation deal with this problem?

First, mediation makes no pretense that it can directly answer this question for the parties. Mediation posits that the parties themselves already have the answer to this question as part of their life experience. The task of mediation is to guide them in a process of discovering how the question is to be answered.

Second, there are certain general principles which can be useful to the parties, during their journey of discovery. These are the guidelines established in the Marital Mediation Rules defining marital property, spousal maintenance, child support, and child custody and visitation. These guidelines are agreed upon by the parties by their adoption of the Marital Mediation Rules. They are considerably more specific and clear than the statutes of most states. The guidelines were, in fact, derived from an examination of state laws that provided the clearest statement of these principles.

Parties may also ask, "How is it possible for me to reach a settlement without having had legal advice?" And another question: "Is the mediator a lawyer and will he give me legal advice?"

To answer the second question first, the mediator is not a lawyer and will not provide legal advice. The mediator through his training and in the observation of the Marital Mediation Rules is able to provide all the guidance needed for helping a couple arrive at the general conditions of a settlement agreement. The mediator is trained to facilitate cooperative negotiations between the parties, while attorneys, from their training as advocates, are accustomed to the use of competitive bargaining tactics. The advisory attorney in the mediation process does provide legal advice and drafts the settlement agreement, in legal form, based upon the general conditions arrived at by the parties and the mediator. In other words, mediation brings to the parties the highest and best skills of both the mediator and the attorney.

"What is the result of the mediation process?"

Most couples reach settlement in mediation. Settlement means that the parties have in hand a written, detailed, settlement agreement which is legally binding upon them. This is the end result of mediation. It is possible that the parties may reach an impasse in mediation which will have to be resolved by an arbitrator. This is a separate part of the process. From FMA's experience to date, the need for arbitration is rare.

The parties may live separately under the agreement, it may be made an order of the court, or it may become a part of the final judgment and decree in divorce. Like all contracts, it may also be rescinded in its entirety or modified by mutual agreement of the parties. If either party should seek a divorce at any time during the life of such an agreement, it would automatically become, according to its own terms, a part of the final judgment and decree of divorce. Thus, with such a settlement agreement, the process of obtaining a divorce becomes a simple, ministerial act involving minimal costs.

All parties have a legal right to represent themselves in any legal action. A heightened awareness of this right has motivated a growing number of persons to seek and successfully obtain their own divorces. The FMA and mediation centers do not provide do-it-yourself divorce services, but they will refer couples with mediated settlements to an attorney who will handle the divorce on a low-cost basis.

As a final question, parties may wish to know, "How does the cost of a mediated settlement plus divorce compare with employing an attorney and going through the adversarial legal system?"

An exact calculation of costs in either system is simply not possible because no one can predict in advance how much time will be required and what difficulties will be experienced by the parties in reaching settlement. In mediation, all charges incurred are on the basis of an agreed hourly rate. Further, the parties are personally present during all hours used except those few hours in which the attorney is drafting the settlement agreement. In mediation, the couple is asked to make an advance cost deposit sufficient to cover ten hours of mediation time. To date, our experience is that most couples settle in less than this period of time and receive refunds covering the unused time. The advisory attorney in mediation seldom spends more than a total of six hours, which covers his/her attendance at two mediation sessions and the time required for drafting the settlement agreement in the office. Advisory attorneys charge according to previously agreed hourly rates.

By contrast, matrimonial attorneys practice as advocates in an adversarial legal system. The Canons of Ethics under which they practice do not permit an attorney advocate to represent more than one party. Additionally, he or she is prohibited from giving the opposite party any legal advice whatever. It is, of course, not uncommon for a couple to have only one attorney. In such cases, however, the attorney has no obligations at all to the unrepresented party. Most attorneys do not publish fee schedules and are usually not willing to limit themselves, in their representation of matrimonial clients, to an hourly basis. When charges are made on an hourly basis, the range is from $50 to $125 per hour.

More commonly, a retainer fee is charged after the first conference if the attorney is to be employed. The average retainer fee in matrimonial matters is $500. It is unusual for an attorney to refund any part of a retainer fee regardless of what services are rendered. It is generally understood that the retainer fee is sufficient to cover a so-called uncontested divorce, which may include a simple settlement agreement drafted by the attorney on the basis of information supplied by the parties. If controversies arise between the parties, or if the attorney considers that the parties' agreement is not in the "best interests" of his/her client, further negotiations will be required. The retainer fee does not cover these additional negotiations, and at this point a second attorney representing the other party may be required.

In FMA's experience, most settlements are reached after initial disagreements between the parties and do require negotiations. Considering the way the two systems work, as just described, it seems safe to conclude that mediation is more financially advantageous than the adversarial legal system. As has been indicated already, however, financial costs are not the only consideration. The event of divorce does claim both an emotional and financial toll, but the costs to the parties and the family following the divorce can be far more significant. Preliminary research studies by the Department of Social Psychology of Columbia University indicate that the postdivorce relationship of the couple and family for mediated couples is significantly better than for couples who have been divorced through the adversarial legal system. In-depth controlled research is under development, but certainly client reports to the FMA support this finding.

Appendix FMA-B
Orientation, Part II
Explanation of the
Process and the Marital
Mediation Rules

When you come in for your mediation, the first thing that you will notice is that an audiotape recording is being made by the mediator. He or she will explain to you that recording is a normal part of our procedures called for by the rules and is done for the following reasons.

1. Mediation is an impartial process. Making a record of everything that happens throughout the process is the best way of ensuring that both parties and the mediators are following the mediation rules.

2. Occasionally it is useful to turn back the tape so as to clarify what has been previously agreed upon.

3. Research of the mediation process will be continuing at least for the next five or ten years. It is important for future development and training of mediators to better understand what takes place in mediation sessions and discover means by which the process can be improved. Detailed analyses of mediation sessions are needed for this research.

4. The Family Mediation Association will make spot checks of all work being done by mediators operating under its certification.

As will be seen from the audiotape release which authorizes use of the tapes for research, all uses are under conditions which maintain the strictest confidentiality for the parties. Researchers are furnished only case numbers, and not the names of the parties, unless the parties have previously agreed to be interviewed by a researcher.

You may have questions you would like to ask about mediation and the mediation process. You are encouraged to ask for any information you wish about the process *before* you begin working toward reaching settlement. When your questions have been answered, there will be a general explanation as to how mediation works.

First, you will be offered a contract to be signed by yourself and your spouse and the mediation service (in the rules called "center") under which you agree to reach settlement under the Marital Mediation Rules which are a part of the contract. Second, arrangements will be made for you to make a cost deposit covering ten hours of mediation time, plus an estimated amount to cover the hourly charges of your impartial advisory attorney. Mediation rates are published by the mediation service or center. Hourly rates for attorneys will vary, but the rate charged by the attorney selected must be agreeable to you as a condition for his or her employment.

Since the Marital Mediation Rules form a part of the contract, it is important that you read and understand them. Here is a simplified explanation of the rules.

Section 1 Agreement of Parties to Mediate. This means that mediation is a voluntary process which is entered into by written agreement of the parties.

Section 2 Mediation of Future Disputes under Contract Provisions. When parties are already divorced or have a settlement agreement which calls for mediation, this section establishes the procedure for initiating mediation.

Section 3 Scope of Mediation. Marital mediation is not available for every controversy the parties might have, but only these things may be mediated: those related to division of property; custody of minor children including visitation, child support, spousal maintenance; as well as the cost of mediation, arbitration, if necessary, and attorney's fees.

Section 4 Mediation Situations. There are three kinds of situations in which marital mediation is used:

1. When the husband and wife intend to live separately, but are undecided about divorce
2. When they are planning to get a divorce
3. When they are already divorced and need to revise some part of the divorce decree

Section 5 Administrator. The administrator is a center authorized by FMA to perform mediation under its rules. The administrator performs certain functions in the mediation, such as receiving the fee deposit; appointing mediators, arbitrators, and impartial advisory attorneys; and being a common channel for communications between the parties, mediators, attorneys, and arbitrators.

Section 6 Panel of Marital Mediators. FMA is responsible for training, certification, and upgrading the training of its marital mediators. It maintains panels of qualified mediators.

Section 7 Appointment of Mediator. Whenever there is to be a mediation, the center will appoint a mediator.

Section 8 Number of Mediators. Unless one of the parties wants two mediators, there will be only one. If there are two, one must be a man and the other a woman. Two mediators, of course, increase the cost of mediation.

Section 9 Qualifications of Mediators. The mediator appointed must be neutral in dealings with the parties. If he or she has had any relationship with either party which might raise a presumption of bias, or if he should have any financial interest in the outcome of the mediation, he would be disqualified.

Section 10 Vacancies. If the mediator is not serving for any reason, the center can declare a vacancy and appoint another.

Section 11 Appointment of Advisory Attorney. The parties may select an advisory attorney from the panel of the FMA or may select any other attorney of their choice, provided he agrees to abide by the rules relating to advisory attorneys. During mediation, the attorney is not involved in the negotiations leading up to the parties reaching a settlement. Legal skill is required for translating the basic agreement of the parties into a legal document which is clear and workable and maximizes tax advantages for the family. The advisory attorney typically spends less time with the parties than the mediator, but his role in the process is no less important.

Section 12 Obligations of the Advisory Attorney. This section is intended to define the advisory attorney's role for his own understanding and that of the parties. The provisions of this section represent part of the parties' contract with the attorney. No effort will be made to summarize these provisions, since a summary would be about as long as the provisions themselves.

Section 13 Compensation of Mediators. The rules require that the mediator's hourly rate be approved by FMA and be acceptable to the parties before mediation begins.

Section 14 Certification and Supervision of Centers. Centers offering mediation service can contract for certification and supervision by FMA.

Section 15 Mediation Fee Deposit. A deposit sufficient to cover ten hours of mediation time and advisory attorney's fees may be required by the center.

Section 16 Refund of Deposit. The unearned portion of the deposit mentioned in the preceding section *will be refunded under all the following conditions:*

1. When the parties have reached settlement
2. If the parties become reconciled or disabled
3. When the parties reach impasse and have proceeded with arbitration.

However, *the deposit will not be refunded if the parties fail to proceed with mediation after ten days' notice to do so.*

Section 17 Communications with Mediators and Advisory Attorneys. This means that the parties are not to talk with either the mediator or the advisory attorney outside of mediation sessions at which both parties are present. It may be necessary for a mediator to contact a party directly about changing or canceling an appointment, and this is permitted. The same rules apply to the advisory attorney.

Section 18 Cancellation of Appointments. The mediator's time, allocation of space and facilities, and sometimes the advisory attorney's time as well are involved when a mediation session is scheduled. Unnecessary costs are incurred if the parties fail to give the center 24 hours' notice of cancellation of an appointment so that time and facilities can be reallocated. Thus when 24 hours' notice is not given, full charge will be made.

Section 19 Attendance at Mediation Sessions. In mediation, it is important that a certain momentum be maintained. Weekly two-hour appointments have been found to produce the best results. Parties agree under this section to arrange their affairs to meet such a schedule.

Section 20 Determination of Impasse. Impasse means that the parties simply cannot or will not agree upon a particular issue. An impasse may be declared:

1. By the mediator at any time
2. By a party if the mediator agrees with him
3. By a party regardless of the mediator's agreement after ten hours of mediation

Section 21 Confidentiality of Mediation. Everything that happens in mediation is confidential and may not be used for any other purpose except as provided for in the research release. In particular, neither party may use against the other disclosures made during mediation through use of tape recordings, the center's files, or the testimony of the mediator. The specific wording of this section is intended to evoke provisions of law which support the objectives just stated.

Section 22 Tape Recording of Mediation Sessions. The provisions of this section were discussed at the beginning of this explanation.

Section 23 Full Disclosure. In order for the parties to make rational decisions, full and complete financial information must be available to them.

Consequently, all relevant information regarding income and financial holdings must be disclosed.

Section 24 Preparation of Budgets. If parties are to reach agreement on the basis of needs, it is essential that they shall have made a sufficient analysis of their needs that they can discuss them rationally. It is also easier to reach agreement on the individual parts of a budget, one at a time, than on general statements of needs. When a party has not made such an examination of needs, the conduct of a mediation session is most likely to be counterproductive. The mediator may decide to discontinue the session rather than proceed. Unless sufficient reasons are given for not having prepared a budget, full charge will be made.

Section 25 Participation of Children and Others. This section refers primarily to working out issues relating to custody and visitation. While the rules do not require that the children participate, the couple is strongly urged to allow their participation if, in the judgment of the mediator, they are old enough to generally understand what is taking place. "Other parties" refers to other significant persons living in the household.

Section 26 Third-Party Involvement. Once mediation has begun, it is important that the parties not discuss mediation sessions with outside persons. It is impossible for such persons to know all the facts and to fully appreciate what is going on in mediation. Consequently, if consulted, they are prone to give advice which has a high likelihood of being counterproductive. At times it comes as a welcome relief to the parties when they learn from this rule that they are not even to discuss matters in mediation with each other outside of sessions. Doing so can sometimes lead to bitter disputes which result in a considerable setback in the process of reaching settlement. At times, the mediator will assign tasks for the couple to carry out jointly when it appears that they can do so without serious risks.

Section 27 Temporary Custody and Support—Arbitration. At the first mediation session, the parties will be expected to enter into a temporary agreement providing for custody and support. The agreement remains in effect only so long as the mediation is in progress. If the couple should fail to do this promptly, then arbitration of this issue will be scheduled and the arbitrator will make a decision by which both parties are bound. Part of this agreement will call for either closing charge accounts or limiting their use to one party with an agreement as to who shall be responsible for present balances and future charges. Agreement is also reached regarding jointly held assets like checking or savings accounts.

Section 28 Transfers of Property. During mediation it is important that no significant transfers of property be made except by mutual agreement of the parties after disclosure of all conditions of the transfer. This rule is intended to form a basis for legal action by the injured party in the event the other party should make transfers without his consent and full disclosure.

Section 29 Temporary Court Order. The temporary agreement provided for in Section 27 may be made an order of court if either party should feel the need to have this done. No notice need be given to the opposite party of such action.

Section 30 Guidelines for Division of Property. These provisions are complex and should be read carefully by the parties. They define marital property as being all the property acquired by the couple during the course of the marriage without regard to which of them holds legal title. Generally speaking, property which was owned by either party prior to the marriage or was received during the marriage by gift or inheritance is excluded.

Section 31 Spousal Maintenance Guidelines. Here *spousal maintenance* refers to that maintenance which is required by the dependent spouse. Under the mediation rules this may be either the husband or the wife but, by force of social custom, the dependent spouse is most often the wife. The term *spousal maintenance* replaces what was once called *alimony*. The reason for using a new term is because it follows a different concept. Generally the following principles apply:

1. It is determined according to the support need of the dependent spouse and the ability of the supporting spouse to provide it.

2. It is not determined on the basis of an assessment of fault on the part of either party.

3. During an initial period of time it may include an increased level of support so that the dependent spouse may make the transition from dependency to self-sufficiency.

4. Payments may include specific amounts for training intended to increase the skills and ability of the dependent spouse to become self-supporting.

5. While complete self-sufficiency is the general aim of spousal maintenance, it also takes into account that the dependent spouse may suffer from a long-term or permanent disability because of age, physical condition, sex, or having simply been out of the job market for many years. Such disabilities are rarely total. The allocation to the dependent spouse of marital property is also a factor which will influence the level of support (especially long-term support) needed.

Section 32 Child Support Guidelines. While some states impose this responsibility solely on the father, the parties are encouraged to share this responsibility between the two parents (and most states provide for this).

Section 33 Child Custody Guidelines. This rule, which is meant to provide guidelines for determining which of the parents will be the custodial parent, follows the so-called best-interest principle. If we assume both parents want custody of the children, then to reach a decision when, as is most usual, both parents are equally well qualified defies rational resolution. In considering the wishes of the children, care must be taken so as not to place them in the position of feeling that they are rejecting one parent. Handling such situations with sensitivity is one of the more important parts of the mediator's training.

Section 34 Rights of the Custodial Parent. The parties are encouraged to reach agreement regarding decisions involving the children. But when agreements are not reached, the custodial parent has the power to make the decision.

Section 35 Rights of the Noncustodial Parent. These provisions are aimed at avoiding having the noncustodial parent become the rejected parent. Even though there has been a divorce, and even though the children are living most of the time with one parent, they still have two parents. It is important in the postdivorce relationship that the responsibilities of parenting continue to be shared by the parents.

Section 36 Rights of Joint Custodial Parents. *Joint Custody* is a relatively new and controversial concept. Most state laws neither provide for it nor specifically prohibit it. No judge will order it against the wishes of the parties, and some may refuse to sanction it even when the parties wish to have this arrangement. It has been included in the rules as an option for parties to consider on the basis of research conducted by Dr. Melvin Roman. The results of this research will be published in his book, *The Disposable Parent,* in the latter part of 1978. The findings indicate that when couples place themselves in a relationship with each other (joint and equal authority) which requires cooperation, they cooperate with each other. This contrasts with the relationship created by designating one parent as custodial parent and giving that parent final authority to make decisions. It has been demonstrated time and again how designating one parent as the ultimate authority figure in divorce proceedings sets the stage for years of controversy.

As to what arrangement is in the best interests of the children, we agree with those authorities who say that the relationship between the parents is by far the most significant factor. We are not unmindful of the importance of the child's peer relationship in a neighborhood or school, or of his need for a certain stability in life, life-style, and living arrangements. All these and other relevant factors should be taken into account in working out living arrangements, even when there is joint custody.

Joint custody does not mean that the children will live for equal lengths of time with each parent or that there will be constant movement back and forth between them. When parents agree upon a joint-custody arrangement, a lawful civil contract has been established even if the court will not enforce it and if, against their wishes, it designates one of them custodial parent. The parties may still decide to share parental responsibility rather than the arrangement the court has imposed on them. In practice, many parents are doing exactly this without a court order calling for joint custody.

Section 37 Controversy over Custody. If the parties are not in agreement as to which shall be the custodial parent, this issue should be announced by the parties at the orientation. The parties can then be assigned the task of developing two budgets. This means that each party makes a first budget, assuming that he is the custodial parent, including his needs and those of the children. Then a second budget is made, assuming that he is the non-custodial parent, omitting from that budget the children's needs. Each party includes in his budget the support he will provide for the children. Mediation will then proceed until all financial issues are resolved between the parties. After this is reduced to a signed agreement, mediation of the custody issue will continue until a decision is reached. Typically, in the custody portion of the mediation, the mediator will ask that the parties first agree as to visitation arrangements for the noncustodial parent in advance of deciding who will be the custodial parent. These procedures are aimed at avoiding having the children become financial pawns and having ill will between the parties acted out around the issue of visitation.

Section 38 Agreement on Issues during Mediation. The mediator has the power to open and close issues. Once the parties have agreed upon an issue, the mediator will declare it closed. It will not be reopened unless the mediator believes there is a valid reason for doing so. If the parties were allowed to leave each issue open for further negotiation, mediation could go on indefinitely without resolution.

Section 39 Execution of Settlement Agreement. This section provides for specific circumstances or points in mediation at which the signing of a settlement agreement is required. Usually this is when the parties have agreed upon all issues or if there is a controversy over custody, all issues except that issue.

Section 40 Evaluation of Settlement Agreement. This provision has been included in the rules in response to the need many parties have expressed that a third party given them reassurance that their contract is workable and is generally consistent with what others have done. Since negotiating such an agreement is a first, and hopefully last, such experience for most parties, their feeling such a need is understandable. Nonconcurrence of the mediator, provided for in Section 41, will be exercised in the more extreme situations and therefore does not replace the more definitive evaluation offered under this section.

The opinions of the mediator and advisory attorney may vary, as opinions among experts often do. However, unlike that of outside experts, their opinions are based upon the detailed information they have gained in working with the parties. While most mediators and advisory attorneys will not welcome this task, FMA has concluded that this resource should be available to parties who ask for it.

As in other areas of life in which there is little in the way of concrete evidence to support opinion, everyone tends to become an expert, usually under two conditions: it is another person's problem, and it is *after* that person has made a decision. There are few subjects in which the personal bias of the expert plays such a significant role as in divorce settlements and in which after-the-fact opinions are expressed with more fervor. Further, because mediation is a fairly new process, some experts may have an investment in finding fault with the results. Some persons attempt to build up their own egos by making another person feel foolish.

It is for these reasons that the evaluations of the mediator and the advisory attorney are offered as an alternative to evaluations of outside parties. Evaluation will be given only if requested by a party before the settlement agreement is signed. In requesting evaluation, a party should be aware that, as a result, either he or the other party may wish to have revisions made in the agreement. If the revisions are minor and are agreed upon by the parties, the mediator will allow them to be made during the evaluation session. If there is disagreement or the revisions require further negotiations, the mediator may schedule further mediation session.

Section 41 Concurrence of Mediators. When the parties have reached a final agreement, the mediator's concurrence indicates that in his judgment it is a fair agreement. If the mediator does not consider it a fair agreement in some respects, then it is his duty to enter his nonconcurrence on the agreement. Neither the mediator's concurrence nor nonconcurrence will affect the legality of the agreement reached by the parties. The mediator's nonconcurrence signals to the parties that, in the mediator's view, a fair agreement has not been reached. In FMA's experience, it has been rare that a mediator has had to suggest nonconcurrence, but when this has been done, the parties then worked out a more equitable agreement. Further, FMA, the center, and the mediator may take this means to disassociate themselves from an agreement that they consider unfair.

Section 42 Arbitration. In the event the parties reach impasse over any issue as provided under Section 20 of these rules, it will be resolved by arbitration under the Marital Arbitration Rules which follow the same guidelines as those provided in the Marital Mediation Rules. They are designed to provide a procedural structure for the arbitration process. Arbitration, unlike mediation, is an adversarial process in which each party can present his own case or be represented by counsel. Each party may offer witnesses and documentary evidence. After hearing from both parties, the arbitrator will make a decision that is binding upon them both. FMA's experience is that arbitration is rarely required. FMA or the center will furnish a copy of the arbitration rules at the request of either party and answer questions that the parties have concerning them.

Section 43 Masculine and Feminine Gender. When the English language develops a unisex personal pronoun, this section can be eliminated. Until then, *he* is intended to mean *he* or *she* unless the context indicates otherwise.

Section 44 Interpretation and Application of the Rules. If the parties and the mediator are not able to reach agreement regarding interpretation of the rules, the center or FMA will make a final decision.

Section 45 Amendment of the Rules. FMA may amend the rules at any time, but such amendments do not affect mediations in progress.

Assuming that you are satisfied to proceed with mediation, you may now turn to the contract form which is entitled "Mediation-Arbitration Agreement." The only blanks in this contract are those which indicate the number of mediators and fees to be paid. This information will be provided for you.

After you have signed this agreement, please look over the budget and financial information forms which are included in your packet. These are to be completed in triplicate and brought to the first mediation session. You have two copies of the form. One is intended as a work copy, and the other is to be completed in final form from which two Xerox copies can be made. At the first session, one copy will become a part of the mediator's file, and the other will be furnished to your spouse.

Appendix FMA-C
Marital Mediation
Rules

Section 1 Agreement of Parties to Mediate. The parties shall be deemed to have made these rules a part of their mediation agreement whenever their agreement so provides or whenever they have agreed in writing that mediation shall be conducted by a facility certified by the Family Mediation Association. These rules and any amendment thereof shall apply in the form obtaining at the time the mediation is initiated. Certified facilities are hereinafter referred to as "Center," and Family Mediation Association as "FMA."

Section 2 Mediation of Future Dispute under Contract Provision. A provision for mediation under these rules in either an antenuptial contract or a settlement agreement may be initiated in the following manner:

a. The initiating party may give notice to the opposite party of his intention to mediate, which notice shall contain a statement setting forth the nature of the dispute including the amount involved, if any, and the remedy sought, and

b. By filing with a center two copies of said notice together with two copies of the mediation provisions of the contract.

c. The center serving as administrator shall give further notice of such filing to the opposite party. If the opposite party so desires, an answering statement in duplicate may be filed with the center, in which event a copy of the answering statement shall be sent to the initiating party by the center. If the opposite party fails to file an answer, mediation shall proceed at a time and place fixed by the center not earlier than ten days after mailing a notice to both parties.

Section 3 Scope of Mediation. Any mediation process constituted by the parties under these rules, unless otherwise stipulated, shall be related to fostering settlement and resolving controversies between them concerning one or more of the following matters, to wit: division of property; custody of minor children including visitation, child support, spousal maintenance; cost of mediation and arbitration; and attorney's fees.

Section 4 Mediation Situations. Mediation under these rules shall be applicable in the following situations.

a. When the parties are husband and wife and have reached a decision to live separately.

b. When the parties are husband and wife, have reached a decision to live separately, and either one or both parties have decided on, or are considering the dissolution of their marriage. The decision to dissolve or not dissolve the marriage shall not be an issue for mediation.

c. When the parties are divorced and a controversy exists between them regarding modification of a previous decree of the court and it is contended that there has been a change of circumstances justifying such modification.

Section 5 Administration. When parties agree to mediation under these rules, and designate a certified center, they thereby constitute the center as the administrator of the mediation. The authority and obligations of the administrator are prescribed in these rules. In the event the parties shall fail to agree upon or designate a particular center, FMA shall designate a center as administrator, and its decision shall be final and binding.

Section 6 Panel of Marital Mediators. The FMA shall establish and maintain certified panels of marital mediators from which mediators shall be appointed.

Section 7 Appointment of Mediator. Upon receipt of notice of intention to mediate under Section 2 or under an agreement under Section 1, the center shall appoint a mediator or mediators for the parties.

Section 8 Number of Mediators. Mediation shall be conducted by a single mediator, unless either party shall request that there be two mediators before the first mediation session. In the event two mediators are requested, one shall be male and the other shall be female.

Section 9 Qualifications of Mediators. Mediators shall be neutral in their relationship to the parties and shall disclose to the center any circumstances likely to affect their impartiality, including any bias or circumstances likely to create a presumption of bias, or any financial or personal interest in the result of the mediation or any past or present relationships with either of the parties or persons closely related to them. Upon receipt of such information from the mediator or other source, the center shall communicate such information to the parties and, if it deems appropriate to do so, to the mediator. Either party or the mediator may request that he be replaced at any time, giving the center reasons therefore. The center shall determine whether a mediator should be disqualified or replaced and shall inform the parties of its decision which shall be conclusive.

Section 10 Vacancies. If any mediator should resign, die, withdraw, refuse appointment, be disqualified, or for any other reason shall fail to consistently perform the duties of his office, the center may declare the office vacant. Vacancies shall be filled in accordance with the rules regarding appointment of mediators.

Section 11 Appointment of Advisory Attorney. The parties may select from FMA's panel of approved attorneys an advisory attorney at law with whom arrangements can be made to provide impartial legal advice needed for reaching settlement. The parties may also select any other attorney mutually acceptable to them, provided he acknowledges in writing appointment as an impartial advisory attorney under these rules and agrees to abide by them in serving the parties. The center shall appoint an advisory attorney from the panel upon the failure of the parties to make a selection or at their request. The advisory attorney shall be compensated at an hourly rate acceptable to the parties in advance of appointment.

Section 12 Obligations of Advisory Attorney. The advisory attorney, by accepting appointment, undertakes the following obligations:

a. He will advise the center and the parties of any circumstance which might create a presumption of bias on his part in favor of or against either party.
b. He will under no circumstances accept professional or other employment, or the promise thereof, from either party so long as their marital dispute is unresolved and during a period of one year thereafter. By mutual agreement of the parties, he may represent one of them for the sole purpose of obtaining a decree of separation or divorce which incorporates the settlement agreement reached by the parties under these rules.
c. He will, as fully as possible within the time available, explain to each party in the presence of the other party and the mediators his and her rights and obligations under the law.
d. He will give particular attention to the tax consequences resulting from the various options available to the parties in reaching settlement.
e. He will maintain strict impartiality in his advice to the parties and will refrain from attempting to influence either party toward making a particular decision or settlement.
f. After preparation of a settlement agreement, he will fully and impartially explain its terms to each party in the presence of the other and the mediators, and will answer questions to the best of his professional abilities.
g. He will communicate with the parties only in mediation sessions or through the center or the mediators and in no other manner directly or indirectly. Further, he will immediately report to the mediators any at-

tempt on the part of a party to communicate with him and advise the party of his obligation.

h. He shall make known to the parties and mediators in advance the maximum number of hours of professional time he expects to render outside of mediation sessions for preparation of the settlement contract or legal research.

i. An advisory attorney may spend only the number of professional hours authorized by the parties.

j. He shall have an attorney-client relationship with the parties and will regard all communications and information obtained during mediation as privileged.

k. The motivations of the parties in reaching a decision to separate or to dissolve their marriage are matters to be dealt with by marriage counselors or other properly qualified therapists and do not come within the purview of the mediation and arbitration processes.

Section 13 Compensation of Mediators. Each mediator shall be compensated at an hourly rate not exceeding that approved by the center under FMA policies and which is acceptable to the parties.

Section 14 Certification and Supervision of Centers. Centers offering mediation under these rules may arrange with FMA for certification and supervision during certification.

Section 15 Mediation Fee Deposit. Upon filing of the agreement for mediation under these rules (Section 1 or 2), the center may require that the parties deposit an amount of money sufficient to cover the following items:

a. Ten hours for mediator's fees
b. An additional estimated amount from which the advisory attorney's fees and/or paraprofessional legal services may be paid

During the mediation process, as the deposit becomes depleted, the center may require that the parties make additional deposits so as to maintain adequate funds needed to continue the mediation process without interruption.

Section 16 Refund of Deposit. The unused portion of deposits provided for in the preceding section shall be refundable to the parties as follows:

a. When settlement has been reached and executed in writing by the parties.
b. If, during mediation, a party becomes permanently disabled or de-

ceased or the parties become reconciled and resume their marital relationship.

c. When impasse has been reached, as provided in Section 20, and the parties are proceeding with arbitration.

d. In the event the parties shall fail or refuse to proceed with mediation and/or arbitration after ten (10) days' written notice has been mailed to them, all deposits remaining become the property of the center and FMA in equal shares.

Section 17 Communications with Mediators and Advisory Attorney. The parties shall not communicate with the mediators or advisory attorney concerning matters in mediation except in the presence of each other during a mediation session. In the event either party shall violate or attempt to violate this rule, the mediator or attorney shall have the duty to ask such party to refrain from such communication and to thereafter promptly report such communication to the center. Communications regarding the scheduling of appointments are permitted under this section.

Section 18 Cancellation of Appointments. Notice of cancellation of mediation appointments must be given by the parties to the center not less than 24 hours in advance of the appointment. Otherwise full charge may be made for the appointment not kept.

Section 19 Attendance at Mediation Sessions. The parties shall arrange their business and personal affairs so as to provide for attending mediation sessions once each week.

Section 20 Determination of Impasse. *Impasse* is defined as a situation resulting when the parties and the mediators have examined as fully as appears useful all information and options reasonably available for reaching settlement of an issue and the parties fail to reach an agreement. The failure or refusal of one or both parties to abide by these rules shall also constitute an impasse when so determined by the mediator. The mediators or a party may declare that an impasse has been reached as follows:

a. By the mediator at any time.

b. By a party with the concurrence of the mediator in advance of completion of ten hours of mediation time

c. By a party with or without the concurrence of the mediator after completion of ten hours of mediation time

Section 21 Confidentiality of Mediation. By undertaking mediation under these rules, the center and the parties mutually agree with one another as follows:

a. Mediation is a procedure for reaching settlement of a dispute either in litigation or likely to be in litigation between the parties.

b. All communication between the parties and with the mediators and the center related to the dispute shall come within the purview of the rules of evidence which exclude from introduction in evidence by either party against the other disclosure made with a view to settlement.

c. The parties shall be estopped through their adoption of these rules from calling either the mediator or any officer or agent of the center as a witness in litigation of any description in which they are called upon to testify as to any matter regarding the mediation proceeding; and the parties shall be estopped from requiring the production in court of any records or documents or tape recordings made by the mediators or the center.

d. The foregoing exclusions from evidence and exemptions of the mediators and parties from giving testimony or being called upon to produce documents shall apply in the same manner to arbitration of an impasse.

e. Mediations conducted by a licensed professional shall come within the purview of his professional privilege.

Section 22 Tape Recording of Mediation Sessions. The center may require that mediation sessions be recorded subject to the following conditions:

a. In the absence of written consent of the parties, audiotape recordings will be heard only by the parties, the mediator, and the mediator's supervisor if he is subject to supervision.

b. Mediators shall disclose to the parties at the beginning of mediation whether or not the mediation sessions will be subject to audiotape supervision.

c. Except as above stated, audiotape recordings are strictly confidential and shall not be used for research, training, or any other purpose without prior written consent of the parties, and then in such manner as does not disclose the identities of the parties.

d. Videotape recordings shall be made only with the prior written consent of the parties.

Section 23 Full Disclosure. Each party shall fully disclose, in the presence of the other party, all information and writings, such as financial statements, income tax returns, etc., requested by the mediator and all information requested by the opposite party if the mediator finds that the disclosure is appropriate to the mediation process and may aid the parties in reaching settlement.

Section 24 Preparation of Budgets. The preparation of budgets by each party, when either spousal maintenance or child support or both are claimed, is an essential part of the mediation process. If either party shall fail or refuse to prepare a budget adequately reflecting his needs, the mediator shall have the duty to suspend mediation of these issues or, at his discretion, declare an impasse.

Section 25 Participation of Children and Others. Children for whom custodial arrangements are being made and other persons having a direct interest in the mediation may participate in mediation sessions related to their interests, if the mediator finds that their participation may facilitate settlement.

Section 26 Third-Party Involvement. During the mediation process, the parties shall refrain from discussing the matters in mediation with all third parties including friends, relatives, and attorneys, and with each other except as directed by the mediators.

Section 27 Temporary Custody and Support—Arbitration. At the first mediation session the parties will reach agreement, if possible, with regard to temporary custody and temporary support for the minor children, temporary support for the spouse seeking maintenance, attorney's fees, and the cost of mediation and arbitration. In the event the parties shall not reach agreement in whole or in part, the mediators shall declare that the parties are in impasse. Upon notification by the mediators that the parties are in impasse, the center shall appoint a single arbitrator who will fix a time and place for hearing not later than seven days after impasse is declared and, after hearing from each party who appears, shall render an award fixing temporary spousal maintenance, temporary custody and support of minor children, the cost of mediation, arbitration, and attorney's fees. The agreement reached between the parties, or the award of the arbitrator, and the provisions of Section 28 of these rules may be made an order of the court having jurisdiction upon the petition of either party without further advance notice or service upon the opposite party.

Section 28 Transfers of Property. During the mediation and arbitration process under these rules, neither party shall transfer, encumber, conceal, or in any other way dispose of any tangible or intangible property except in the usual course of business or for the necessities of life. Proposed transactions by either party in the regular course of business or for any other purpose affecting 10 percent or more of the total assets of a party shall be reported to the other party not less than ten days in advance of the transaction contemplated. Transactions made in violation of this rule shall be subject to being declared void and set aside upon the application of the injured party, either in arbitration under these rules or in a court of competent jurisdiction.

Section 29 Temporary Court Order. During mediation or arbitration, either party may request a court of competent jurisdiction to issue a temporary injunction without requiring advance notice to the opposite party:

a. Restraining any party from transferring, encumbering, concealing, or in any way disposing of any property except in the usual course of business or for the necessities of life and, if so restrained, requiring him to notify the moving party of any proposed extraordinary expenditures and to account to the court for all extraordinary expenditures made after the order is issued
b. Enjoining a party from molesting or disturbing the peace of the other party or of any child
c. Excluding a party from the family home or from the home of the other party when there is evidence that physical or emotional harm would otherwise result.

Section 30 Guidelines for Division of Property. The parties shall reach agreement providing for the division of marital property with the assistance of the mediators, without regard to marital misconduct, in such proportions as is just, after considering all relevant factors, including:

a. The contribution of each spouse to the acquisition of the marital property, including the contribution of a spouse as homemaker.
b. The value of the property to be received or retained by each spouse.
c. The economic circumstances of each spouse at the time the division of property is to become effective, including the desirability of awarding the family home or the right to live therein for reasonable periods to the spouse having custody of any children.
d. Any increases or decreases in the value of the separate property of each spouse during the marriage or the depletion of the separate property for marital purposes.
e. For purposes of this section:
   Active ownership of property is inferred from the owner's making capital improvements, usage, management, and other efforts intended to enhance the value of the property.
   Passive ownership is inferred from the absence of factors which would result in an inference of active ownership.
   Marital property means all property acquired by either spouse subsequent to the marriage except:

   (1) Property acquired by gift, bequest, devise, or descent.

   (2) Property acquired in exchange for property acquired by gift, bequest, devise, or descent.

   (3) Property acquired by a spouse after a decree of legal separation.

   (4) Property excluded by valid agreement of the parties

   (5) The increase in value resulting from passive ownership of property acquired prior to the marriage, or after the marriage by gift, bequest, devise, or descent.

   (6) When increases in value of property acquired prior to the marriage, after the marriage or by gift, bequest, devise, or descent have resulted from both active and passive ownership, a reasonable allocation shall be made so as to exclude increases attributable to passive ownership.

f.   All property acquired by either spouse after the marriage prior to a decree of legal separation or divorce and all increases in value attributable to active ownership of property whenever or however acquired, are presumed to be marital property regardless of whether title is held individually or by the spouses in some form of coownership, such as joint tenancy, tenancy in common, tenancy by the entirety, and community property. The presumption of marital property shall be overcome by a showing that the property or increase in value of property is excluded under the provisions of the preceding subsection.

g.   Property shall be valued for purposes of this section as of the date of the first mediation session.

Section 31 Spousal Maintenance Guidelines. Payment of maintenance by one spouse to the other shall be predicated upon the following considerations as they apply to the spouse seeking maintenance:

a.   The spouse lacks sufficient property, including marital property apportioned to him, to provide for his reasonable needs.

b.   The spouse is fully or partially unable to support himself through appropriate employment or is the custodian of a child whose condition or circumstances make it appropriate that the custodian not be required to seek employment outside the home.

c.   Maintenance shall be in such amounts and for such periods of time as is just, without regard to marital misconduct and after considering all relevant factors, including the following:

   (1) The financial resources of the party seeking maintenance, including marital property apportioned to him, and his ability to meet his needs independently, including the extent to which a provision for

support of a child living with the party includes a sum for that party as custodian.

(2) The time necessary to acquire sufficient education or training to enable the party seeking maintenance to find appropriate employment

(3) The standard of living established during the marriage, reduced by the impact that maintaining two households rather than one may have upon the standard of living of the parties

(4) The duration of the marriage

(5) The age and physical and emotional condition of each spouse

(6) The ability of the spouse from whom maintenance is sought to meet his needs while meeting those of the spouse seeking maintenance

Section 32 Child Support Guidelines. Either parent or both parents, according to their ability to do so, shall accept the duty of support for a child of the marriage and contribute an amount reasonably necessary after considering all relevant factors, including:

a. The financial resources of the child
b. The earning ability and financial resources of each parent
c. The standard of living the child would have enjoyed had the marriage not been dissolved, reduced by the impact that maintaining two households rather than one may have upon the standard of living of the parties
d. The physical and emotional condition of the child and his educational needs

Section 33 Child Custody Guidelines. In reaching agreement regarding custodial arrangements reflecting the best interests of the child, the parties shall consider all relevant factors, including:

a. The wishes of each parent as to the custody of the child
b. The wishes of the child as to custodial arrangements
c. The interaction and interrelationship with his parent or parents, his siblings, and any other person who may significantly affect the child's best interests
d. The child's adjustment to his home, school, and community
e. The mental and physical health of all individuals involved

The conduct of a parent that does not demonstrably affect his relationship with the child, or in some other way can be shown to be contrary to the best interests of the child, shall not be considered.

Section 34 Rights of the Custodial Parent. The custodial parent may determine the child's upbringing, including his education, health care, and religious training, except as otherwise agreed by the parties. The custodial parent shall have the right to require that the noncustodial parent follow agreed visitation with the children on a consistent and dependable basis.

Section 35 Rights of the Noncustodial Parent. The noncustodial parent of the child shall be entitled to reasonable visitation rights such as do not adversely affect the child's education or physical health or significantly impair his emotional development. The noncustodial parent shall carry out visitation arrangements as a privilege and obligation of parenthood and to share parenting responsibility with the custodial parent.

Section 36 Rights of Joint Custodial Parents. Joint custodial parents agree to establish a cooperative relationship with each other regarding the exercise of their continuing responsibilities as parents of their children. They accept that each has an equal right to determine the child's upbringing, including his education, health care, and religious training. The child's living arrangements between the two parents shall be such as are in the best interests of the child, using as guidelines the provisions of Section 33 of these rules. Even though joint custody reflects a cooperative attitude on the part of both parents, specific living arrangements shall be included in the settlement agreement. Such arrangements shall be followed except as are otherwise agreed upon by the parents from time to time. The living arrangements contained in the settlement agreement shall not be changed by such subsequent agreements. Either parent on notice to the other may reestablish the arrangements contained in the settlement agreement.

Section 37 Controversy Over Custody. At the first mediation session, the mediators shall determine whether the parties are in agreement regarding custody of the minor child or children. In the event custody of the children is in controversy, the mediator shall advise the parties that mediation of the custody issue shall be the last item on the agenda after agreement has been reached upon all the following:

a. Division of marital property
b. Spousal maintenance
c. Child support
d. Attorney's fees for the petitioning spouse when the parties contemplate dissolution of their marriage.

The mediator shall further instruct each party to prepare two budgets—one based upon the assumption that he is the custodial parent and a second based upon the assumption that he is the noncustodial parent.

Section 38 Agreement upon Issues during Mediation. As agreement is reached upon each issue during mediation, the mediator shall determine that the parties understand the agreement reached. Thereafter, the same issue shall not be reopened for mediation, after a new issue is taken up, without authorization by the mediator. The mediator shall grant authorization to reopen mediation of an issue to the extent needed to correct mistakes or to consider new information which was not reasonably available to one or both parties previously.

Section 39 Execution of Settlement Agreement. The advisory attorney shall personally supervise the execution of the settlement agreement reached by the parties during mediation. Such agreement shall be prepared and submitted to the parties when one of the following situations arises:

a. The parties have reached settlement of all issues.
b. The parties have reached settlement of all issues except custody (including visitation) which will require further mediation.
c. The parties have reached settlement of some issues and are in impasse over others, in which case the agreement shall reflect the issues agreed upon and shall clearly specify the position of each party regarding issues in impasse.
d. The parties are in impasse over all issues, in which case the agreement shall clearly specify the position of each party in each issue.
e. The failure or refusal of either party to enter into the agreement provided for in Subsections c and d shall not limit the other's right to proceed with arbitration.
f. A supplemental or revised agreement shall be executed reflecting custodial arrangements agreed upon after further mediation, as provided for in Subsection b above.

Section 40 Evaluation of Settlement Agreement. In advance of their execution of the settlement agreement, either party may request that a special evaluation session be scheduled. At such evaluation session, the mediator and the advisory attorney shall offer the parties their opinions as to the overall workability of the proposed agreement, pointing out the advantages and disadvantages to each party. To the best of their ability and on the basis of their previous experience, the mediator and attorney shall indicate whether the agreement is substantially consistent with agreements reached by couples similarly situated.

Section 41 Concurrence of Mediators. The mediators may indicate to the parties their concurrence or nonconcurrence with the settlement agreement reached. A written notation of the mediators' concurrence or nonconcurrence shall be made below the signatures of the parties on the settlement agreement and shall be signed by the mediators. Concurrence indicates the mediator's judgment that the settlement appears to be substantially equitable and fair to each party. Nonconcurrence shall in no way detract from the legal effectiveness of the settlement contract reached between the parties.

Section 42 Arbitration. The parties shall submit to arbitration all controversies which are the subject of mediation under these rules when impasse is reached under Section 20 of these rules. Arbitration shall be conducted under the Marital Arbitration Rules of the FMA and in accordance with applicable statutory arbitration laws of the state in which the arbitration is conducted. The parties accept the jurisdiction of the court competent to handle divorce cases, in the place where the arbitration is conducted for all purposes related to the conduct of the arbitration, such as compelling the attendance of witnesses and production of documents. The parties shall faithfully observe this provision for arbitration and the arbitration rules, so that the award rendered by the arbitrators shall become a part of the settlement agreement reached between the parties, and/or that such award may be entered in and made the judgment of any court having jurisdiction thereof.

Section 43 Masculine and Feminine Gender. Whenever in these rules the masculine gender is used, it shall be understood to include the feminine unless the context clearly indicates otherwise.

Section 44 Interpretation and Application of Rules. The mediator shall interpret and apply these rules. In the event of a controversy between the mediator and the parties regarding interpretation or application of these rules, such questions shall be referred to the center for a decision which, however, shall be subject to review by FMA.

Section 45 Amendment of Rules. FMA reserves the right to amend these rules at any time, provided, however, such amendment shall not apply to the rules included in mediation agreements relating to existing controversies. The rules as amended and in force at the time notice of intention to mediate is given under Section 2 shall apply in mediations under agreements to mediate future disputes.

Appendix FMA-D
Marital Arbitration
Rules

Section 1 Agreement of Parties. The parties shall be deemed to have made these rules a part of their arbitration agreement whenever they have provided for arbitration by the Family Mediation Association, Inc., hereinafter designated FMA, or under its rules. These rules and any amendment thereof shall apply in the form obtaining at the time the arbitration is initiated.

Section 2 Administrator. When parties agree to arbitrate under these rules and an arbitration is initiated thereunder, they thereby constitute FMA the administrator of the arbitration. The authority and obligations of the administrator are prescribed in the agreement of the parties and in these rules.

Section 3 Delegation of Duties. The duties of the FMA as administrator under these rules may be carried out through such officers or agents as it may designate.

Section 4 National Panel of Arbitrators. The FMA shall establish and maintain a national panel of marital arbitrators and shall appoint arbitrators therefrom as hereinafter provided.

Section 5 Arbitration of Existing Controversy. Parties to any existing dispute may agree to arbitration under these rules by filing with FMA two copies of a written agreement to arbitrate under these rules signed by the parties. It shall contain a statement of the matter in dispute and the remedy sought, together with the appropriate cost deposit.

Section 6 Contract Provision for Arbitration. Arbitration under these rules is initiated in the following manner:

a. The initiating party shall give notice to the opposite party of his intention to arbitrate. The notice shall contain a statement setting forth the nature of the dispute and the remedy sought.

The Family Mediation Association, Inc., acknowledges the contribution of the American Arbitration Association (AAA) in the development of arbitration rules over the last fifty years. Many of the general concepts included in these rules were developed by AAA. FMA has adapted these concepts to marital controversy and added provision for impartial legal service, guidelines for property division, support, and custody. An early draft of these rules was furnished to AAA in March 1976. Some of FMA's concepts have been included in AAA's "Family Dispute Services."

131

b. The initiating party shall file with FMA two (2) copies of said notice, and two (2) copies of the contract including arbitration provisions, together with the appropriate cost deposit.

The FMA shall give notice of such filing to the opposite party. If he so desires, the opposite party may file an answering statement in duplicate with FMA within seven days after notice from FMA, and shall simultaneously send a copy of his answer to the initiating party. Failure to file an answer shall not operate to delay the arbitration.

Section 7 Scope of Arbitration. Any arbitration under these rules shall be related to the settlement of controversies between the parties about one or more of the following matters:

a. Division of marital property
b. Custody of minor children including visitation
c. Child support
d. Spousal maintenance
e. Cost of mediation (when applicable) and arbitration
f. Attorney's fees

Section 8 Fixing of Locale. The parties may mutually agree on the locale where the arbitration is to be held. If the locale is not designated by the parties within seven days from the date of filing the notice, the FMA shall have power to determine the locale. Its decision shall be final and binding.

Section 9 Qualifications of Arbitrator. Any arbitrator appointed pursuant to Section 10 shall be neutral and subject to disqualification for the reasons specified in Section 13. If the agreement of the parties names an arbitrator or specifies any other method of appointing an arbitrator, or if the parties specifically agree in writing, such arbitrator shall not be subject to disqualification for said reasons.

Section 10 Appointment from Panel. Immediately after the filing of the notice, the FMA shall submit simultaneously to each party an identical list of names of persons chosen from the panel. Each party shall have seven days from the mailing date in which to cross off any names to which he objects, number the remaining names indicating the order of his preference, and return the list to FMA. If a party does not return the list within the time specified, all persons named therein shall be deemed acceptable. From among the persons who have been approved on both lists, and in accordance with the designated order of mutual preference, the FMA shall invite the acceptance of an arbitrator to serve. If the parties fail to agree upon any of the persons named, or if for any reason the appointment cannot be made from the submitted list, FMA shall make the appointment from the other members of the panel without the submission of any additional lists.

Section 11 Number of Arbitrators. If the arbitration agreement does not specify the number of arbitrators, the dispute shall be heard and determined by one arbitrator, unless FMA, in its discretion, or state law directs that a greater number of arbitrators be appointed.

Section 12 Notice to Arbitrator of His Appointment. Notice of the appointment shall be mailed to the arbitrator or arbitrators by FMA, together with a copy of these rules, and the signed acceptance of each arbitrator shall be filed prior to the opening of the first hearing.

Section 13 Disclosure and Challenge Procedure. A person appointed as neutral arbitrator shall disclose to FMA any circumstances likely to affect his impartiality, including any bias or any financial or personal interest in the result of the arbitration or any past or present relationship with the parties or their counsel. Upon receipt of such information from such arbitrator or other source, FMA shall communicate such information to the parties and, if it deems it appropriate to do so, to the arbitrator and others. Thereafter, FMA shall determine whether the arbitrator should be disqualified and shall inform the parties of its decision, which shall be conclusive.

Section 14 Vacancies. If a neutral arbitrator should resign, die, withdraw, refuse, be disqualified, or be unable to perform the duties of his office, the FMA may, on proof satisfactory to it, declare the office vacant. Vacancies shall be filled in accordance with the applicable provisions of these rules, and the matter shall be reheard unless the parties shall agree otherwise.

Section 15 Time and Place. The arbitrator shall fix the time and place for each hearing within the locale fixed under Section 8. FMA shall mail to each party notice thereof at least five days in advance, unless the parties by mutual agreement waive such notice or modify the terms thereof.

Section 16 Representation by Counsel. Any party may be represented by counsel. A party intending to be so represented shall notify the other party and FMA of the name and address of counsel at least three days prior to the date set for the hearing at which counsel is first to appear. When an arbitration is initiated by counsel, or where an attorney replies for the other party, such notice is deemed to have been given.

Section 17 Stenographic Record. The FMA shall make the necessary arrangements for the taking of a stenographic record or audiotape recording whenever requested by a party. The requesting party or parties shall pay the cost of such record or recording and shall deposit with FMA an amount estimated by FMA to cover the cost thereof.

Section 18 Adjournments. The arbitrator may take adjournments upon the request of a party or upon his own initiative and shall take such adjournment when all the parties agree.

Section 19 Oaths. Before proceeding with the first hearing each arbitrator may take an oath of office and, if required by law, shall do so.

Section 20 Majority Decision. Whenever there is more than one arbitrator, all decisions of the arbitrators must be made by at least a majority. The award must also be made by at least a majority.

Section 21 Order of Proceedings. A hearing shall be opened by the filing of the oath of the arbitrator where required, and by recording the place, time, and date of the hearing, the presence of the arbitrator and parties, and counsel, if any, and by the receipt by the arbitrator of the notice and answer, if any. The initiating party shall then present his claim and proofs and his witnesses who shall submit to questions or other examination. The opposite party shall then present his proofs and his witnesses who shall submit to questions or other examination. The arbitrator may determine which is the initiating party in the event the notice or agreement does not specify, and in his discretion may vary this procedure, but he shall afford full and equal opportunity to all parties for the presentation of any relevant material or proofs.

Exhibits, when offered by either party, may be received in evidence by the arbitrator.

The names and addresses of all witnesses and exhibits in order received shall be made a part of the record.

Section 22 Arbitration in the Absence of a Party. Unless the law provides to the contrary, the arbitration may proceed in the absence of any party who, after due notice, fails to be present or fails to obtain adjournment. An award shall not be made solely on the default of a party. The arbitrator shall require the party who is present to submit such evidence as he may require for the making of an award.

Section 23 Evidence—Excluding Marital Misconduct. Except for evidence of marital misconduct, the parties may offer such evidence as they desire and shall produce such additional evidence as the arbitrator may deem necessary to an understanding and determination of the dispute. When the arbitrator is authorized by law to subpoena witnesses or documents, he may do so upon his own initiative or upon the request of any party. The arbitrator shall judge the relevancy and materiality of the evidence offered, and conformity to legal rules of evidence shall not be necessary. All evidence shall be taken in the presence of all the arbitrators and all the parties, except where any of the parties is absent in default or has waived his right to be present.

Section 24 Full Dislosure of Assets. When controversies over property division or support are submitted the arbitrator shall require that both parties produce all information and writings reasonably required so as to provide a full and complete statement of assets and liabilities, including financial statements presently prepared and previously furnished to others, income tax returns, bank statements, and all other information requested by opposing parties of the other party if the arbitrator finds such information is relevant and reasonably contributes to the parties making full disclosure of assets and liabilities.

Section 25 Preparation of Budgets. When either spousal maintenance and/or child support is to be determined by the arbitrator, each party shall be required to prepare and introduce into evidence a budget or budgets reflecting his needs as directed by the arbitrator.

Section 26 Evidence by Affidavit and Filing of Documents. The arbitrator shall receive and consider the evidence of witnesses by affidavit, but shall give it only such weight as he deems it is entitled to after consideration of any objections made to its admission.

All documents not filed with the arbitrator at the hearing but arranged for at the hearing or subsequently by agreement of the parties shall be filed with the FMA for transmittal to the arbitrator. All parties shall be afforded opportunity to examine such documents.

Section 27 Inspection or Investigation. Whenever the arbitrator deems it necessary to make an inspection or investigation in connection with the arbitration, he shall direct the FMA to advise the parties of his intention. The arbitrator shall make a verbal or written report to the parties and afford them an opportunity to comment.

Section 28 Transfers of Property. During arbitration under these rules, neither party shall transfer, encumber, conceal, or in any other way dispose of any tangible or intangible property except in the usual course of business or for the necessities of life. Proposed transactions by either party in the regular course of business or for any other purpose affecting 10 percent or more of the total assets of the party shall be reported to the opposite party not less than ten (10) days in advance of the transaction contemplated. Transactions made in violation of this rule shall be subject to being declared void and set aside upon the application of the injured party either in arbitration under these rules or in a court of competent jurisdiction.

Section 29 Temporary Custody, Support, and Applicability of Rules. Within seven (7) days after his appointment, the arbitrator, at the request of either party or upon his own initiative, may fix a time and place for a preliminary hearing upon either or both of the following matters:

a. Temporary support for the minor children of the parties, if any; temporary support for the spouse seeking maintenance; attorney's fees; temporary custody of the minor children of the parties; and the cost of arbitration.

b. Upon his own initiative or upon the application of either party, the arbitrator shall rule upon the applicability of these rules, respecting spousal maintenance and division of marital property when it appears or is contended by either party that they are in conflict with the public policy of the state.

Section 30 Temporary Court Order. During arbitration, either party may request a court of competent jurisdiction to issue a temporary injunction without advance notice to the opposite party which may provide for:

a. Restraining any party from transferring, encumbering, concealing, or in any way disposing of property in a manner contrary to that prescribed in Section 28 of these rules and requiring the party to account to the court for all extraordinary expenditures made after the order is issued

b. Enjoining a party from molesting or disturbing the peace of the other party or of any child

c. Excluding a party from the family home or from the home of the other party when there is evidence that physical or emotional harm would otherwise result

Section 31 Temporary Court Order for Custody and Support. Upon application of either party, the arbitrator's award regarding temporary custody, support, and other costs as provided in Section 29 of these rules may be submitted to the court for its approval, and entry of an order making such ruling of the arbitrator an order of the court.

Section 32 Conflicts with State Law/Public Policy. The arbitrator shall follow these rules rather than local law with respect to all matters relating to division of marital property and spousal maintenance except to the extent any provision herein shall be against the public policy of the state in which enforcement of the arbitrator's award will be sought. In the event any provision herein shall be contended by either party to be against the public policy of the state, he shall notify the opposite party and the FMA of this contention at least seven days in advance of the first hearing. Such notice shall clearly specify how these rules conflict with public policy and what local law is applicable in lieu thereof. Failure of a party to so notify the FMA and the opposite party shall constitute a waiver of his right to object upon the ground that these rules are violative of the public policy of the state. In the event the arbitrator shall find that local law prevails over these rules as herein provided, he shall notify the parties and the FMA of the parts of the rules affected and the local law which shall be followed during the conduct of the arbitration.

Section 33 Arbitrator's Award Upon Custody and Child Support. The arbitrator's award shall be subject to the approval of the court respecting custody and child support. Without attempting to limit the court's right of inquiry into these matters, the parties agree by their adoption of these rules that the arbitrator's award shall be submitted to the court without reopening these issues. The court may, in its discretion, enter the arbitrator's award in the same manner as a consent order submitted by the parties.

Section 34 Closing of Hearings. The arbitrator shall specifically inquire of all parties whether they have any further proofs to offer or witnesses to be heard. Upon receiving negative replies, the arbitrator shall declare the hearings closed. If briefs are to be filed, the hearings shall be declared closed as of the final date set by the arbitrator for the receipt of briefs. If documents are to be filed as provided for in Section 26 and the date set for their receipt is later than that set for the receipt of briefs, the later date shall be the date of closing the hearing. The time limit within which the arbitrator is required to make his award shall commence to run, in the absence of other agreements by the parties, upon the closing of the hearings.

Section 35 Reopening of Hearings. The hearings may be reopened by the arbitrator on his own motion, or upon application of a party at any time before the award is made. The arbitrator shall have 30 days from the closing of the reopened hearings within which to make an award.

Section 36 Waiver of Rules Violation. Any party who proceeds with the arbitration after knowledge that any provision or requirement of these rules has not been complied with, and who fails to state his objection thereto in writing, shall be deemed to have waived his right to object.

Section 37 Extension of Time. The parties may modify any period of time by mutual agreement. The FMA for good cause may extend any period of time established by these rules, except the time for making the award. The FMA shall notify the parties of any such extension of time and its reason therefor.

Section 38 Communication with Arbitrator and Serving of Notices

a. There shall be no communication between the parties and a neutral arbitrator except at hearings. Any other oral or written communications from the parties to the arbitrator shall be directed to the FMA for transmittal to the arbitrator.
b. Each party to an agreement which provides for arbitration under these rules shall be deemed to have consented that any papers, notices, or process necessary or proper for the initiation or continuation of an arbitration under these rules and for any court action in connection therewith or for the entry of judgment on any award made thereunder may be served upon such party by mail addressed to such party or his attorney at his last known address or by personal service.

Section 39 Compensation of Arbitrator. Each neutral arbitrator shall be compensated at an hourly rate not exceeding that approved for such arbitrator by FMA and which is acceptable to the parties.

Section 40 Guidelilnes for Division of Marital Property. Marital property shall be divided between the parties, without regard to marital misconduct, in such proportions as is just after considering all relevant factors, including:

a. The contribution of each spouse to the acquisition of the marital property, including the contribution of a spouse as homemaker.
b. The value of the property to be received or retained by each spouse.
c. The economic circumstances of each spouse at the time the division of property is to become effective, including the desirability of awarding the family home or the right to live therein for reasonable periods to the spouse having custody of any children.
d. Any increases or decreases in the value of the separate property of each spouse during the marriage, or the depletion of the separate property for marital purposes.
e. For purposes of this section:

Active ownership of property is inferred from the making of capital improvements, usage, management, and other efforts intended to enhance the value of the property.

Passive ownership is inferred from the absence of factors which would result in an inference of active ownership.

Marital property means all property acquired by either spouse subsequence to the marriage except:

(1) Property acquired by gift, bequest, devise, or descent.
(2) Property acquired in exchange for property acquired by gift, bequest, devise, or descent.
(3) Property acquired by a spouse after a decree of legal separation.
(4) Property excluded by valid agreement of the parties.
(5) The increase in value resulting from passive ownership of property acquired prior to the marriage, after the marriage, or by gift, devise, or descent.
(6) When increases in value of property acquired prior to the marriage, after the marriage, or by gift, bequest, devise, or descent, have resulted from both active and passive ownership, a reasonable allocation shall be made so as to exclude increases attributable to passive ownership.

f. All property acquired by either spouse after the marriage and prior to a decree of legal separation or divorce, and all increases in value attributable to active ownership of property whenever or however acquired are presumed to be marital property, regardless of whether title is held individually or by the spouses in some form of co-ownership, such as joint tenancy, tenancy by the entirety, and community property. The presumption of marital property shall be overcome by showing that the property or increase in value of property is excluded under the provisions of the preceding subsection.

g. Property shall be valued for purposes of this section as of the date of the first mediation session under the rules of FMA, where applicable, or the date on which arbitration is initiated under Section 6, when mediation has not preceded arbitration.

Section 41 Spousal Maintenance Guidelines. Payments of maintenance by one spouse to the other shall be without regard to marital misconduct and shall be predicated upon the following consideration as they apply to the spouse seeking maintenance:

a. The spouse lacks sufficient property, including marital property apportioned to him, to provide for his reasonable needs.
b. The spouse is fully or partially unable to support himself through

appropriate employment or is the custodian of a child whose condition or circumstances make it appropriate that the custodian not be required to seek employment outside the home.

c. Maintenance shall be in such amounts and for such period of time as is just without regard to marital misconduct after considering all relevant factors, including the following:

  (1) The financial resources of the party seeking maintenance, including marital property apportioned to him, and his ability to meet his needs independently, including the extent to which a provision for support of a child living with the party includes a sum for that party as custodian

  (2) The time necessary to acquire sufficient education or training to enable the party seeking maintenance to find appropriate employment

  (3) The standard of living established during the marriage and the impact that maintaining two households rather than one may have on the standard of living of the parties

  (4) The duration of the marriage

  (5) The age and physical and emotional condition of each spouse

  (6) The ability of the spouse from whom maintenance is sought to meet his needs while meeting those of the spouse seeking maintenance

Section 42 Child Support Guidelines. Either parent or both parents shall accept the duty of support for a child of the marriage and pay an amount reasonable or necessary after considering all relevant factors, including:

a. The financial resources of the child
b. The earning ability and financial resources of each parent
c. The standard of living the child would have enjoyed had the marriage not been dissolved, reduced by the impact that maintaining two households rather than one may have upon the standard of living of the parties
d. The physical and emotional condition of the child and his educational needs

Section 43 Child Custody Guidelines. Custody of the minor children of the parties shall be determined in accordance with the best interests of the child and shall take into consideration all relevant factors, including:

a. The wishes of each parent as to the custody of the child
b. The wishes of the child as to custodial arrangements
c. The interaction and interrelationship with his parent or parents, his siblings, and any other person who may significantly affect the child's best interests

d. The child's adjustment of his home, school, and community
e. The mental and physical health of all individuals involved

The arbitrator shall not consider the conduct of a parent that does not demonstrably affect his relationship with the child or in some other way can be shown to be contrary to the best interests of the child.

Section 44 Controversy over Custody. In the event custody of the children is in controversy, the arbitrator may in his discretion conduct his hearing upon this issue separately, after he has heard evidence on all other matters submitted to him, including the following:

a. Division of marital property
b. Spousal maintenance
c. Child support
d. Attorney's fees for the petitioning spouse when the parties contemplate dissolution of their marriage
e. Cost of arbitration and attorney's fees

In the event the arbitrator shall defer hearing evidence on the issue of custody until after he has concluded his hearing upon the preceding items, he shall require that each party prepare two budgets—one based upon the assumption that he is the custodial parent and a second based upon the assumption that he is the noncustodial parent.

Section 45 Participation of Children and Others. Children or other persons having a direct interest in the arbitration shall be entitled to participate in hearings related to their interests. The arbitrator shall have the power to require the retirement of any witness or witnesses during the testimony of other witnesses. It shall be discretionary with the arbitrator to determine the propriety of the attendance of any person, including parties, during his examination of children regarding their custody.

Section 46 Appointment of Advisory Attorney. The parties may agree upon or select from the FMA panel of approved attorneys an advisory attorney at law following the rendition of the award by the arbitrator. The arbitrator's award upon issues previously at impasse shall be combined with other matters on which the parties are in agreement, so that a final settlement agreement may be prepared. The advisory attorney shall carefully follow the award rendered by the arbitrator and previous agreements reached between the parties, so as to construct a legal instrument which can be incorporated into the divorce decree and serve as an ongoing guide for the parties in their postseparation or divorce relationship.

The advisory attorney may suggest to the parties ways for following the arbitrator's award and their previous agreements which offer the best prospects for a cooperative relationship with each other and a supportive environment for the children. Alternative ways of following the arbitrator's award and previous agreements may be considered which will maximize tax savings.

In no event shall the advisory attorney allow the parties to depart from prearbitration agreements or the award of the arbitrator. The advisory attorney shall be compensated at an hourly rate that is acceptable to the parties.

Section 47 Obligations of an Advisory Attorney. The advisory attorney, by accepting appointment, undertakes the following obligations:

a. He will advise the FMA and the parties of any circumstance which might create a presumption of bias on his part in favor of or against either party.

b. He will under no circumstances accept professional or other employment, or the promise thereof, from either party prior to their execution of a final settlement agreement and during a period of one year thereafter.

c. He will give particular attention to the tax consequences resulting from various options available to the parties within agreements previously reached by them and the arbitrator's award, without deviating from the substance thereof.

d. He will maintain strict impartiality in his advice to the parties.

e. After preparation of the final settlement agreement, he will fully and impartially explain its terms to each party and will answer questions to the best of his professional ability.

f. He will communicate with the parties only in the presence of each other or through the FMA and in no other manner directly or indirectly. He will further immediately report to the FMA any attempt on the part of a party to communicate with him and advise the party of his obligation.

g. The number of hours of professional time he expects to render outside of his meetings with the parties for preparation of the settlement contract or legal research shall be made known to the parties in advance and authorized by them.

h. His role as an attorney is strictly advisory, and he is not an advocate for either party.

i. The motivations of the parties in reaching decisions presented to him and the award of the arbitrator and the emotional or psychological or other consequences to themselves or their children are matters which do not come within the purview of the advisory attorney's professional or personal responsibility.

Section 48 Time of Award. The award shall be made promptly by the arbitrator and, unless otherwise agreed by the parties or specified by law, no later than 30 days from the date of closing the hearings.

Section 49 Form of Award. The award shall be in writing and shall be signed either by the sole arbitrator or by at least a majority if there is more than one. If shall be executed in the manner required by law.

Section 50 Scope of Award. The arbitrator may grant any remedy or relief which he deems just and equitable and within the scope of these rules. The arbitrator, in his award, shall assess arbitration fees and expenses between the parties and, in the event any administrative fees or expenses are due the FMA, shall make an award covering such items in favor of FMA.

Section 51 Award of Settlement. If the parties settle their dispute during the course of the arbitration, the arbitrator, upon their request, may set forth the terms of the agreed settlement in an award.

Section 52 Delivery of Award to Parties. Parties shall accept as legal delivery of the award the placing of the award or a true copy thereof in the mail by the FMA, addressed to such party at his last known address or to his attorney, or personal service of the award, or the filing of the award in any manner which may be prescribed by law.

Section 53 Release of Documents for Judicial Proceedings. The FMA shall, upon the written request of a party, furnish to such party, at his expense, certified facsimiles of any papers in the FMA's possession that may be required in judicial proceedings relating to the arbitration.

Section 54 Applications to Court
a. No judicial proceedings by a party relating to the subject matter of the arbitration shall be deemed a waiver of the party's right to arbitrate.
b. The FMA is not a necessary party in judicial proceedings relating to the arbitration.
c. Parties to these rules shall be deemed to have consented that judgment upon the arbitration award may be entered in any court having jurisdiction thereof.

Section 55 Administrative Fees. The FMA shall prescribe an administrative fee schedule and a refund schedule to compensate it for the cost of providing administrative services. The schedule in effect at the time of filing shall be applicable. The administrative fees shall be deposited with FMA by the parties, subject to final apportionment by the arbitrator in his award.

Section 56 Arbitrator's Fee. Arrangements for the compensation of an arbitrator shall be made through the FMA and not directly by him with the parties.

Section 57 Deposits. The FMA may require the parties to deposit in advance such sums of money as it deems necessary to defray the expense of the arbitration, including the arbitrator's fee, and shall render an accounting to the parties and return any unexpended balance.

Section 58 Interpretation and Application of Rules. The arbitrator shall interpret and apply these rules insofar as they relate to his powers and duties. When there is more than one arbitrator and a difference arises among them concerning the meaning or application of any such rules, it shall be decided by a majority vote. If that is unobtainable, either an arbitrator or a party may refer the question to the FMA for final decision. All other rules shall be interpreted and applied by the FMA.

Section 59 Masculine and Feminine Gender. Whenever in these rules the masculine or feminine gender is used, it shall be understood to include the other gender unless the context clearly indicates otherwise.

Section 60 Amendment of Rules. The FMA reserves the right to amend these rules at any time, provided, however, such amendment shall not apply to existing controversies which have been submitted for arbitration on the date of such amendment.

Appendix FMA-E
A Guide for
Negotiating and
Drafting Marital
Settlement Agreements

This checklist is intended for use by trained marital mediators as an aid in directing the parties' negotiations. Provisions are suggested which are believed to contribute positively to the ongoing family relationship. Attorneys may use it as a means of developing an agreement which meets the needs of the parties. Some areas indicated by this guide will not be applicable to families of moderate means. Implementation of provisions, particularly involving tax consequences, requires skilled wording and current legal research by the drafter. This guide is not meant to replace the need for such research and skill of draftsmanship.

1. Names of parties
   Addresses of parties
2. Names of children
   Birth dates of children
   Ages of children
   No children
3. Recital of marriage
   Date of marriage
   Place of marriage
4. Separation
   Date of separation
   Cause of separation
   Expectation of continued separation
5. Intention of settlement by this agreement
   a. Issues to be settled
      (1) Division of property and debt settlement
      (2) Spousal support (alimony)
      (3) Child support
      (4) Custody and visitation
   b. Avoidance of controversy
   c. Best interests of children
6. Relationship between parties
   a. Each free to live separately as though unmarried
   b. No molestation or effort to compel cohabitation by either party

7. Indebtedness
   a. Between the parties
      (1) Acknowledgment of existence
      (2) Provision for payment
      (3) Security for payment
      (4) Nonexistence of debt or negate nonscheduled debt
   b. Due third parties—individually incurred
      (1) Payable by husband
      (2) Payable by wife
      (3) Indemnity of each against third-party claims resulting from failure to pay
      (4) Undisclosed debt assumed by party incurring
   c. Recovery of specific property loaned
   d. Property of spouse pledged to secure debt of other spouse
   e. Joint obligations to third parties, options:
      (1) Continued joint obligation
      (2) Assumed by one party
      (3) Indemnity to nonassuming party
8. Personal property
   a. Household goods
      (1) Attach memoranda listing property owned by each and where located.
      (2) Provide for physical division and removal. Advance notice to party in possession. Final date for removal.
   b. Jewelry and works of art
   c. Stocks, bonds, and notes receivable
   d. Automobiles, boats, motorcycles, bicycles, cameras, hobby equipment, etc.
   e. Animals, pets, and potted plants
   f. Merchandise credits
   g. Club memberships
   h. Partnership interests
   i. Bank accounts, savings accounts, brokerage accounts, and accounts receivable
   j. Goods in storage—payment of accrued charges
   k. Insurance on personal property
      (1) List by owner
      (2) Designate parent responsible for management of minor's property
   l. Contents of safe deposit boxes
   m. Income tax refunds anticipated
   n. Vested interests in trusts, retirement plans, and wife's social security coverage after twenty years of marriage
   o. Warranty of full disclosure by each party

9. Real property
  a. Divesting inchoate dower right (some states)
    (1) May be released by settlement agreement (some states)
    (2) May be divested by conveyance to third parties and reconveyance to one party (some states)
  b. Rights of creditors
    (1) Husband or wife as creditor as to third parties
    (2) Transfers in fraud of third-party creditors
    (3) Reliance of third party upon settlement agreement as to non-fraudulent transfers
  c. Transfers and retention of title
    (1) Absolute transfers to a party
    (2) Absolute retention of title by a party
    (3) Transfers to a party with beneficial interest to children
    (4) Retention of title with beneficial interest to children
    (5) Transfers of life or limited-term interest and remainder provision
    (6) Retention of life or limited-term interest and remainder provision
  d. Jointly owned property or property to be divided
    (1) Right to occupancy—term
    (2) Obligations of parties
    (3) Provision for sale or division
      (a) Earliest date for sale
      (b) Sales price or method for determining
      (c) Costs of sale
      (d) Division of proceeds
      (e) Failure to find buyer within stipulated time
    (4) Notification to opposite party of failure to meet any obligation respecting property, including:
      (a) Payment of mortgage obligations
      (b) Payment of *ad valorem* taxes
      (c) Maintenance of casualty insurance
      (d) Maintenance required for preservation of property
      (e) Vacancy of property over 30 days
  e. Ownership of personal property related to real property maintenance, e.g., lawn mowers, ladders, tools, stocks of seed and fertilizer, miscellaneous implements
  f. Effect of reconciliation on
    (1) Executory provisions
    (2) Executed provisions
  g. Reliance upon party's warranty as to ownership and existence of liens against property

h. Right to occupancy of leased property
   (1) Conditions
   (2) Obligations of parties
10. Custody of child or children
   a. Designation of one party as custodial parent
   b. Less frequent options to designation of one parent as custodial parent:
      (1) Joint custody—each parent has equal voice in decisions, even though child may reside more time with one than the other
      (2) Divided custody—substantial division of time spent with each parent, with each having full control while child is in his or her custody
      (3) Split custody—when there are several children and some are to be in custody of one parent and the remainder in the custody of the other
   c. Recital that arrangements are deemed to be in the best interests of the children, followed by supporting reasons
   d. Acknowledgment of fitness of both parties and that both continue to have responsibilities as parents
      (1) Definition of role of custodial parent
      (2) Definition of role of noncustodial parent
      (3) Agreement to cooperate and support each other in respective parenting roles
      (4) Establishment of consistent pattern in identifying and dealing with children's
         (a) Needs (essential support provisions)
         (b) Wants (enrichment and "extras")
   e. Wishes of child or children
      (1) As to custody at age when choice can be exercised (age 11, 14, or 16 depending on state law)
      (2) If one or more children have attained age of choosing custodial arrangements, recite that they have been consulted and that agreement follows wishes of child
      (3) Agreement that when child reaches age to choose, he may exercise choice with full permission of both parents
   f. Visitation with noncustodial parent—a sharing of parental responsibility
      (1) Obligatory scheduled visitation
         (a) Indicate whether all children or less than all and how determined
         (b) Specify beginning and ending of visitation periods by day and hour
         (c) Advance notice of circumstances requiring change in scheduled visitation

      (d) Provision for alternative custodial arrangements (babysit-ter) paid for by noncustodial parent when that parent does not comply with scheduled visitation

    (2) Additional discretionary visitation to be scheduled by advance notice and agreement of parties and children

    (3) Geographical limitations requiring prior agreement of custodial parent when exceeded

    (4) Visitation related to events such as national holidays, religious holidays, birthdays, graduations, weddings, serious illness, and death of a family member (e.g., parent, grandparent, aunt, and uncle)

    (5) Extended visitation related to annual vacation

    (6) In the event of accident or onset of serious illness while child is in the custody of either parent, the other shall be immediately notified; also in the event of any other illness requiring confine-ment to bed for more than 24 hours

    (7) Unlimited visitation, subject to medical limitations imposed, shall be allowed noncustodial parent during illness

  g. Custodial and visitation arrangements assume that parties will con-tinue to live within, for example, a 50-mile radius of present loca-tion.

  h. Provide for payment of court costs and attorney's fees

11. Spousal maintenance

  a. Including or not including child support, with beginning date and due date of continuing payments

  b. Fixed sum payable periodically. If more than ten years, tax deduc-tible by paying spouse. Excess over 10 percent paid in any one year, or series of payments over less than ten years are not deductible.

  c. Indefinite periodic payments

  d. Time-limited periodic payments subject to a contingency, e.g., nonremarriage of dependent spouse; may be intended to cover rehabilitative needs of dependent spouse or be related to child support contingencies when child support is included with spousal support

  e. Effect of remarriage of dependent spouse

    (1) Termination of all payments

    (2) Limited continuance of payments as inducement to remarry (probably tax deductible)

    (3) Lump-sum payment on remarriage as inducement (probably not tax deductible)

  f. Modification

    (1) Modifiable or nonmodifiable

    (2) Conditions for modification:

      (a) Increased or decreased needs, income, or resources of dependent spouse

        (b) Increased or decreased needs, income, or resources of supporting spouse

        (c) Economic factors affecting both parties

    (3) Provision for mediation and arbitration of impasse

  g. Supporting spouse precedes in death the dependent spouse

    (1) Payments terminate or continue as obligation of estate

    (2) Payments terminate and fixed sum is payable from estate or life insurance

  h. Warranty of each party that a stated amount of income and resources may be relied upon by the opposite party

  i. Provision for security to ensure payment (e.g., collateral, establishment of a trust)

12. Child support

  a. Payments for children may be included in spousal maintenance

  b. Specify amounts, beginning date, and continuing dates of all payments

  c. Conditions under which payments will cease:

    (1) Attainment of age 18 or majority under state law

    (2) Marriage, child becomes self-supporting, discontinues education for other than health reasons

    (3) Death of child

    (4) Induction into armed forces

  d. Change, if any, of support payments during periods of scheduled visitation

  e. Provision for health care through insurance and for services not covered. Items covered, hospitalization, medical and dental, including orthodontia, glasses, and mental health care by medical or nonmedical professionals

  f. Prior approval required for health service not covered by insurance

  g. Statement as to proportion of child support assumed by each parent

  h. Provision for college education beyond age 18:

    (1) Payments to parent or directly to child

    (2) Limited to state-supported college at in-state rate

    (3) Minimum grade average required

    (4) Bonus grade average payment

  i. Provision for marriage of daughter, bar mitzvah, and similar events in life of child

  j. Provision for security to ensure payment (e.g., collateral, establishment of a trust)

  k. Provision for revision due to changed circumstances with mediation and arbitration of impasse

13. Insurance: life, accident, and health
    a. Carried on life of either or both parties with other or children designated as beneficiaries during children's dependency
    b. Carried on life, accident, and health risks of supporting spouse for benefit of dependent spouse and/or children
    c. Provide for payment of premiums
    d. Specify:
        (1) Type of insurance (Name policy and carrier if presently owned.)
        (2) Ownership of policy
        (3) Conditions under which beneficiary may change
        (4) Duration of coverage
    e. Consider estate tax implications

14. Tax matters
    a. Payments, if deductible by supporting spouse, are taxable as income to dependent spouse
    b. Agree to modify at any time to lower total tax paid by the family without lowering disposable income of either
    c. Allocate support and dependency deductions so as to qualify custodial parent for head-of-household treatment
    d. Consider tax implications
        (1) Alimony trusts and annuities
        (2) Lump-sum settlement (e.g., under ten years or over ten years in periodic payments)
        (3) Life insurance arrangements (premiums may be taxable as alimony and proceeds may be includable in estate for estate tax)
        (4) Legal fees of husband and wife for tax advice are deductible
        (5) Capital gains resulting from transfer of appreciated assets by husband to wife
        (6) Gift taxes resulting from certain conveyances
        (7) Estate tax and income tax aspects of periodic payments to dependent spouse surviving as obligations of estate
    e. Agree whether joint return will be filed
        (1) Provide for signing return
        (2) Provide for division of refund or payment of additional tax
        (3) To be eligible, parties must remain married through end of tax year
    f. Warranty against deficiency assessments on joint returns
        (1) One spouse with all taxable income may warrant against deficiency assessment and hold other harmless against cost of resisting proposed assessment. Property settlement may suggest continuation of joint liability

     (2) Both parties having had income:
- (a) Allocated between parties as to which income or deduction results in deficiency or refund
- (b) Each warrants and holds other harmless as to tax consequences of his income or claimed deductions

g. When payments to spouse are taxable as income and additional payments will be made to approximate taxes:
- (1) Agree as to whether payments will represent first or last portion of spouse's total income
- (2) Dependency allowances to be considered in calculating tax
- (3) Determine whether standard or itemized deductions will be claimed
- (4) Consider whether recipient's losses can be used to offset taxes

h. Agree as to which spouse can use loss carryovers originating under joint return

i. Estate tax deduction:
- (1) Payment for wife's release of support rights may be deductible in some states
- (2) Payment for wife's release of property rights, such as dower, are generally not deductible
- (3) When husband's settlement requires him to leave a part of his estate to his children, the children may be treated as creditors rather than legatees, entitling the estate to a deduction for debt
- (4) Above agreements will be effective only when and if made a part of a decree of divorce or legal separation

15. Attorney's fees—agreed amount as settlement of wife's claim against husband

16. Mutual release of all legal obligations resulting from marriage, limiting future obligations to provisions of agreement

17. Release of claims against estate of each other except as provided in agreement

18. Provision that property settlement and spousal maintenance are reciprocally integrated, each made in consideration of the other, will avoid any change without consent of both parties

19. Provide that agreement will survive and not merge with divorce decree even though incorporated into it

20. Entire agreement—no oral modifications or other agreements. Waiver of breach or default does not alter agreement or right to demand strict compliance.

21. Agreement does not obligate either party to seek a divorce or refrain therefrom, nor does it obligate a party to refrain from defending against the opposite party's application for a divorce

22. Provide that if any provision is held invalid or unenforceable, all other provisions remain in full force and effect
23. Any controversy or claim, including either party's motion to modify the agreement that is not resolved between the parties by mutual consent, shall be submitted to mediation and arbitration under the Marital Mediation Rules of the Family Mediation Association, Inc.

Appendix FMA-F
Settlement Agreement
Provisions

Introduction

The wording in the following settlement agreement is intended to give examples of possible provisions. It is also presented so as to suggest the form an agreement may follow. Some provisions are inconsistent with other provisions. For these reasons the provisions must be thoughtfully selected and adapted so that the needs and agreement of each couple are reflected.

Many couples will not require all these provisions, and simplified provisions may serve even better than some of the detailed examples given. Making the judgment of what is appropriate for each couple requires the legal training and experience of the advisory attorney. These provisions are by no means an exhaustive list of possible provisions. Such a list would be virtually limitless.

Settlement Agreement

STATE OF _____
COUNTY OF _____

This agreement made between JANE DOE of the County of _____, State of _____, hereinafter called the "wife" and JOHN DOE, of the County of _____, State of _____, hereinafter called the "husband";

WITNESSETH:

That the parties hereto were married on or about April 15, 1960, and separated on or about June 20, 1973. There has been issue of the marriage, to wit: JAMES B. DOE, born June 3, 1964; and BETTY B. DOE, born February 6, 1967, the same being hereafter referred to as "children." In consequence of disputes and irreconcilable differences, the parties have heretofore separated and are now living in a bona fide state of separation. In view of their intentions to live apart the rest of their lives, they are desirous of settling their property rights, alimony, maintenance, division of property, custody of and support for the children, and attorney's fees.

NOW, THEREFORE, in consideration of the premises and the mutual undertakings herein contained, the parties do agree as follows:

I.

The parties shall continue to live apart for the rest of their lives. Each shall be free from interference, direct or indirect, by the other as fully as though unmarried. Each may for his or her separate benefit, engage in any employment, business, or profession he or she may choose.

155

II.

The parties shall not molest or interfere with each other, nor shall either attempt to compel the other to cohabit or dwell with him or her, by any means whatsover. This provision and its observance by both parties are of the essence of this agreement and form a part of the consideration for the remaining provisions herein.

Separate Property of the Parties

The parties hereto agree that the husband is now the owner of that property which is described in Exhibit A attached hereto and made a part hereof which is his sole and separate property. The parties further agree that the wife is now the owner of the property scheduled in Exhibit B attached hereto and made a part hereof which property is her sole and separate property. The husband does hereby forever waive any and all rights to the property of the wife scheduled in Exhibit B. The wife does hereby forever waive any and all rights to the property of the husband scheduled in Exhibit A.

Marital Property

The parties hereto agree that all remaining property not scheduled in Exhibits A and B and which is scheduled in Exhibit C attached hereto and made a part hereof is marital property as defined under the Marital Mediation Rules of the Family Mediation Association. Marital property of the parties shall be divided between them in the manner hereinafter provided.

Covenants and Warranties Concerning Other Property

A. Husband hereby warrants that he is not now the owner of any separate property of any kind or description whatsoever, other than such property as is specifically listed in Exhibit A attached hereto, and that he has not made, without knowledge of wife, any gifts or transfers of any property defined as marital property under the provisions of the Marital Mediation Rules of the Family Mediation Association within the past three years. If it shall hereafter be determined that husband is now the owner of any property not set forth in Exhibits A and C attached hereto or that he has made, without disclosing to the wife, any gift or transfer of marital property during the last three years, husband hereby covenants and agrees to pay to wife, on demand, a sum equal to one-half of the net equity at fair market value on the date of transfer of such property reduced by one-half of the proceeds of such sale as husband can show was reinvested in marital property plus all amounts used for family purposes.

B. Wife hereby warrants that she is not now the owner of any property of any kind or description whatsoever other than such property as is specifically listed in Exhibits B and C attached hereto, and that she has not made, without knowledge of husband, any gifts or transfers of any marital property as above defined within the past three years. If it shall hereafter be determined that wife is now the owner of any separate property not set forth in Exhibits B an C or that she has made, without disclosure to the husband, any gift or transfer of marital property during the last three years, wife hereby covenants and agrees to pay husband, on demand, a sum equal to one-half of the fair market value on the date of transfer of such property reduced by one half of the proceeds of such sale as wife can show was reinvested in marital property plus all amounts used for family purposes.

Division of Marital Property

The parties make the following disposition and settlement with respect to their marital property as scheduled in Exhibit C attached hereto representing a division of approximately _____ percent to husband and _____ percent to wife:

A. Husband hereby transfers, conveys, and assigns to wife as her sole and separate property items numbered _____ on Exhibit C attached hereto.

B. Wife hereby transfers, conveys, and assigns to husband as his sole and separate property items numbered _____ on Exhibit C attached hereto.

C. Husband and wife agree that the husband shall have a _____ percent and the wife a _____ percent undivided interest in items numbered _____ on Exhibit C attached hereto.

D. Husband and wife agree that items numbered _____ on Exhibit C shall be sold and the net proceeds be divided between them, _____ percent to husband and _____ percent to wife.

Necessary Instruments

Each party hereto covenants and agrees that he or she shall, upon request, execute, acknowledge, and deliver to the other party herein his heirs, executors, administrators, or other representatives, any and all deeds, contracts, releases, bills of sale, or instruments which may now or hereafter be necessary or convenient to enable the other party hereto to sell or dispose of any property, acquired under or before or after the execution of this agreement.

Right to Dispose of Property

The parties agree that marital property as listed in Exhibit C shall be owned, managed, used, or sold only in the manner provided for in this agreement. All individually owned property listed in Exhibits A and B or which he or she acquires under this agreement, may be owned, managed, used, or sold as fully and effectively as if the parties hereto were single and not married and had never been married.

Power of Attorney

The parties hereto grant to the other a power of attorney to execute their name on any and all bills of sale, deeds, and other documents necessary or convenient to effectuate any of the provisions of this agreement. Said power of attorney granted hereunder shall become operative only in the event that one party has failed to execute any of the aforesaid documents, after first having been given fifteen days' written notice by the other party to do so.

Use and Eventual Disposition of Property

Husband and wife agree that _____ shall have the exclusive right of use of property listed as item _____ Exhibit C, for a term of _____ years after the date of this agreement (without payment of rent) or (and shall pay monthly rent to _____ in the amount of $_____). During such period _____ shall be responsible for payment of insurance, taxes, necessary repairs and maintenance for the preservation of said property, and mortgage payments in the amount of $_____ per month.

At the end of such term the property shall be sold and the net proceeds divided as herein agreed. In the event the property is sold before the end of the term, the net proceeds shall also be divided as herein agreed.

When said property is sold, _____ shall receive the amount of $_____ (plus interest at the rate of _____ percent per annum, compounded annually from the date of this agreement). Payment of said amount shall be secured by a deed of trust or other similar security instrument. The amount payable to _____ above shall represent _____ percent of $_____, which amount is the present fair market value of said property, reduced by the present amounts of the following items:

1. Amounts required to discharge any liens, taxes, judgments, or loans, $_____.
2. Cost of selling property, $_____.
3. Proration of current taxes, $_____.
4. Estimated closing costs and loan discount payable by seller, $_____.

Sale of Property

The parties agree that the homeplace of the parties, item number 1, Exhibit C, located at _____, in _____, _____, shall be offered for sale at a gross sales price of not exceeding $65,000 nor less than $55,000 except by further agreement of the parties. It is agreed that said sale shall be handled by a licensed real estate agent selected by agreement of the parties. In the event the parties cannot agree upon a single agent, they shall draw lots after which the successful party may list the property with an agent of his choice for a period of six months. In the event a firm contract of sale is not obtained during such period of time, then the opposite party may select a different agent who shall likewise undertake to find a purchaser for said property. The net proceeds of the sale shall be divided between the parties according to the percentages set forth in paragraph _____ of this agreement. Net proceeds of sale shall be understood as meaning the gross sales price obtained for sale property reduced by the following:

1. Amounts required to discharge any liens against the property, including loans, judgments, taxes, or other liens established by law.
2. Cost of preparing and maintaining the property in saleable condition
3. Proration of current taxes
4. Proration of prepaid insurance, if assumed by purchaser
5. Closing costs or loan discounts payable by seller
6. Real estate commission
7. Reimbursement to either or both parties for any cash advances made after the property is offered for sale, in connection with any of the foregoing items, including payments required to keep any outstanding loans in current status

Recreational Family Property

The lake property, item _____ on Exhibit C, shall be retained in joint ownership by the parties as long as both parties are satisfied with this arrangement. It is generally understood that the property, if not sooner disposed of, will no longer be needed as a family resource after the last child reaches the age of 18. During joint ownership uses of the property shall be scheduled by agreement between the parties and the children. The cost of all maintenance taxes, insurance, and loan payments shall be borne by each party in accordance with his percentage of ownership as reflected in paragraph _____ hereof.

Collections and Art Objects

The art and coin collections of the parties, items _____, Exhibit C, are difficult to evaluate, although the parties are in agreement that over time these items will enhance in value. It is agreed that the husband shall retain possession of items _____ and the wife shall retain possession of items _____. In the event that either party shall receive what is considered an advantageous opportunity to sell all or a part of said items, the sale will be made if the opposite party agrees. In the event the parties do not reach agreement, either party may then submit the matter for resolution under the FMA Marital Mediation Rules. In the meantime and so long as said property is jointly owned, each party hereby contracts that in the event of his death he will include in his will a bequest of his interest in such property to the children, and the other party may take possession.

Husband-Wife Debt Obligations

The wife hereby acknowledges that she is indebted to the husband in the sum of $10,000, advanced to her by him in connection with the opening of her gift shop. She has delivered to the husband simultaneously herewith her negotiable promissory note repayable in monthly installments of $200 including principal and interest at the rate of 8 percent per annum beginning on the first day of March, 1978, said note being secured by (here describe the security).

Unsecured Creditors

A. Unsecured Marital Obligations. The unsecured marital obligations of the parties are listed in Exhibit D attached hereto and made a part hereof. These obligations shall be paid by the parties according to the same ratios as are established for the division of marital property, paragraph _____. (*Comment:* To the extent such obligations are payable out of liquid marital property, such as saving accounts, provision may be made for their payment from this source. Additionally, provision may be made for payment for such obligations out of the net proceeds of sale of the real estate as an additional deductible item before division is made between the parties. If such resources are not available, then the parties may agree upon an amortization of these obligations out of future income of each party according to his or her percentage of responsibility therefor.)

B. Items listed in Exhibit E attached hereto and made a part hereof are the unsecured obligations of the husband, payment of which are his sole responsibility.

C. Unsecured obligations of the wife. Items listed on Exhibit F attached hereto and made a part hereof are the unsecured obligations of the wife for which she is solely responsible.

If legal action shall be brought against either the husband or the wife to recover any of the above-listed unsecured obligations payable by the other, such party agrees to indemnify said party and hold him or her harmless against such claims and, in addition, to pay all attorney's fees and costs which said party may incur as result of such liability.

Joint Custody

The husband and wife are in agreement that the role of each as a parent must be accorded equal respect and be given equal authority in deciding upon matters relating to the children. They are aware that there will be differences of opinion between them from time to time and that sometimes strong feelings may be involved. These occasions can provide the parents an opportunity to express their feelings and opinions while maintaining basic respect for each other and to model cooperative conflict resolution for their children. The parents are aware, in making this decision for joint custody, of the unresolved differences which led to the decision to dissolve their marital relationship. Despite this decision, they remain committed to each other and the children as parents, and they now reaffirm that commitment.

The parents are agreed that even though custody is joint and equal that the children require a stable home environment and relationship with peers in the neighborhood and at school. For these reasons it is not expected that the children will spend equal time with each parent on a day-to-day basis. With this in mind, it is agreed that the best present living arrangement for the children calls for their having the residence of the _____ as their primary place of abode. This arrangement may be changed by agreement of the parents, but it is further agreed that frequent short-term changes are not in the best interest of the children or parents.

While the children are living with one parent as a primary place of abode, the other parent may have the children visit him/her at all reasonable times and places by agreement with the other parent and the

children. As a general guide to living arrangements which can be relied upon in the absence of any other agreement, the following shall apply:
(here describe the living arrangement)

Custodial Parent

The parties are agreed that each is fully qualified and fit to be the custodial parent for the children while recognizing that it is desirable [and in some states legally required] that one of them serve as custodial parent and the other as noncustodial parent. The _____ shall be the custodial parent, and as such may determine the child's upbringing, including his education, health care, and religious training, except as otherwise agreed by the parties. The custodial parent shall have the right to require that the noncustodial parent follow agreed visitation with the children on a consistent and dependable basis.

Notification and Consultation

Each party shall keep the other advised as to the whereabouts of the children. In the event of a serious injury to or illness of any child (serious illness or injury meaning any injury or illness which may confine the child to bed for more than two days), the party with whom such child may then be shall notify the other party of such injury or illness, and both parties shall have the right to visit such child at all reasonable times during such injury or illness wherever such child may be. Both parties shall have the right to have a physician examine the child. The parties further agree that they will consult with each other and cooperate in making decisions regarding the children and that neither shall do anything to undermine the children's affection and respect for the other.

Noncustodial Parent

The _____ shall be the children's noncustodial parent and as such shall be entitled to visitation rights hereinafter set forth. The noncustodial parent agrees that he will carry out visitation arrangements with the children both as a privilege and as a parenting responsibility shared with the custodial parent. Visitation arrangements shall be as follows:
A. Regular visitation
1. Weekends: _____ shall have the children on alternate weekends from 7:00 p.m. on Friday to 7:00 p.m. on Sunday, commencing Friday, March _____, 1977.

2. Weekdays: _____ shall have the children on alternate Mondays (on the Monday that does not follow his weekend visitation) from 5:30 p.m. to 8:00 p.m., commencing Monday, March _____, 1977.

B. Holidays and special days

1. _____ shall have the children on alternate holidays from 7:00 p.m. on the evening preceding said holiday to 7:00 p.m. on the day of said holiday, holidays being Memorial Day, Independence Day, Labor Day, and Thanksgiving Day, commencing Labor Day, 1977.

2. Christmas: Christmas shall be divided into two periods, the first commencing at 7:00 p.m. on the last day of school before Christmas school vacation and ending at 10:00 a.m. Christmas Day; the second period shall commence at 10:00 a.m. on Christmas Day and terminate at 5:00 p.m. on New Year's Day. Husband and wife shall alternate said periods; _____ shall have the children commencing with the first period in the year 1977.

3. Easter: _____ shall have the children on alternate Easter vacations, commencing in the year 1978, from 7:00 p.m. the last day of school before vacation and ending at 7:00 p.m. the day before school resumes.

4. Father's Day: Husband shall have the children every Father's Day from 11:00 a.m. to 7:00 p.m.

5. Mother's Day: The wife shall have the children every Mother's Day from 11:00 a.m. to 7:00 p.m.

6. Children's birthdays: _____ shall have the children on their birthdays in the year 1978 from 5:00 p.m. to 8:30 p.m. and thereafter on alternate years.

7. Religious holidays:

a. _____ shall have the children on Good Friday from noon to 6:00 p.m. on said day on alternate years commencing with the year 1977.

b. _____ shall have the children on the first day of the Jewish holidays of Yom Kippur, Rosh Hoshana, and Passover, commencing at 5:00 p.m. of the day before and terminating at 7:00 p.m. on such day, on alternate years commencing with the year 1978.

C. Summer Vacation

1. _____ shall have the children during the entire month of July, 1978, the entire month of August the following year, and alternating July and August in subsequent years.

2. _____ (opposite parent) shall have the children on the alternate months of July and August.

D. Priorities

In the event of conflicts in the foregoing schedule, the following priorities are established:

1. Summer vacation as to both parents
2. Holidays and special days as to both parents
3. _____'s regular visitation

E. Miscellaneous

1. The party with the visitation privilege has the responsibility for both picking up and returning the children.

2. In the event the noncustodial parent has visitation on a day contiguous with his weekend visitation, he need not return the child for the intervening night.

3. Neither party shall remove the children from the state of _____ without first having obtained the written consent of the other party.

4. Both parties may maintain reasonable telephone communications with the children.

5. In the event the custodial parent remains at home with the children during that parent's summer vacation month, the noncustodial parent's regular visitation rights shall be observed.

6. Noncustodial parent has the responsibility for the children on all his or her visitation days as herein set forth. The custodial parent is entitled to rely on the same in planning personal activities. In the event of default, the noncustodial parent shall be liable for the reasonable cost of child-care services, payable on demand.

Support

The husband shall make the following payments to the wife for her support and maintenance and for the support, maintenance, and education of the children. As long as child support is payable under any of the following subparagraphs, all payments made shall be for the joint support of the wife and minor children:

A. The sum of $250 per month until the wife dies or remarries, whichever occurs first.

B. In the event the wife shall remarry, the husband shall pay to the wife on the first day of the first month after her marriage the sum of $2000 and the sum of $500 per month on the first day of each month thereafter for a period of six months, commencing one month after said payment of $2000.

C. Husband shall pay to the wife an additional amount of $250 per month until 36 such payments shall have been made, provided, however, such payments shall immediately cease and terminate upon her death or remarriage.

D. In the event either party shall institute suit against the other in a court of competent jurisdiction and the court finds that the husband is liable for payment of attorney's fees, husband shall pay to the wife (or her nominee) as additional support the sum of $_____ or the award of the court, whichever is less.

E. The sum of $250 per month for James B. Doe until he marries, becomes self-supporting, enters military service, becomes 18 years of age, or dies, whichever occurs first.

F. The sum of $250 per month for Betty B. Doe until she marries, becomes self-supporting, becomes 18 years of age, or dies, whichever occurs first.

(The following are alternative child support provisions—payments *not* tax deductible by husband and *not* taxable to wife:)

The husband shall pay to the wife the sum of $_____ per month for the support of the minor children of the parties. The following reduced amounts shall be payable when each child becomes 18 years of age, marries, becomes self-supporting, or dies, whichever occurs first.

1. First child, $_____.
2. Second child, $_____.
3. Last child, $_____.

G. The aforesaid scheduled monthly payments, except as otherwise provided, shall be made in advance, one-half on the fifth day of each month and one-half on the twentieth day of each month, commencing December 5th, 1978.

Life Insurance

Husband agrees that for so long as he shall be legally required to contribute to the support and education of the children, he shall keep a life insurance policy insuring his life in the minimum amount of $_____ in full force and effect, and he shall pay all premiums when due and he shall forthwith designate and confirm the wife (or the children) as the principal beneficiaries of said insurance. Husband further agrees that he shall keep such insurance beneficiary designations in effect until the youngest of the children has attained age 21. If for any reason husband shall no longer have said present insurance policies available to him, then he shall forthwith obtain replacement insurance of a cumulative value of at least $_____ and maintain the same pursuant to the foregoing provisions.

Alternative or Additional Insurance

The husband agrees to provide (or maintain) a minimum of $_____ in unencumbered life insurance on his life with his estate (or _____) named as irrevocable beneficiary. The life insurance policy shall be kept in full force until all obligations required of the husband under this agreement have terminated. To the extent not covered by life insurance, all payments required to be made by the husband shall be first charged against his estate, and the executors, trustees, or personal representatives of the husband's estate are hereby directed to pay such sums prior to the payment of other creditors or beneficiaries of the estate. This agreement shall prevail notwithstanding provisions of the husband's last will and testament to the contrary. At least once each calendar year, the husband shall provide written proof satisfactory to the wife that the foregoing life-insurance policies are unencumbered and otherwise currently in effect.

Provision for Health Needs

During the period when any child is receiving monthly or educational support under the provisions of this agreement, the husband agrees to provide for such child or children medical and hospital insurance equal to that presently carried for the minor children, or a comparable medical and hospital insurance policy maintained by any company by which he is employed. During the time in which the child support payments are required to be made to the wife under the terms of this agreement, the husband agrees that in any calendar year in which the dental or orthodontic payments required to be paid by the wife for the children in her custody exceeds the sum of $100, he will pay any additional expense in excess of said amount incurred during that year.

College Education

After payment of the sums provided for support of each child, the husband shall pay all expenses incurred by each of the children to secure at the earliest opportunity a four-year college education, including books, tuition and fees, room and board, and all other usual and ordinary expenses incident thereto and including transportation to and from home. The college shall be one which shall have accepted the child for admission and is mutually agreed upon by the child and the husband, which agreement shall not be unreasonably withheld. The husband's liability under this paragraph shall be limited to an amount consistent with the costs required for a state resident to attend a state-supported university in the state of residence of the child. In the event the husband shall be obligated for educational payments under this provision while any amounts are still payable by him under the provisions of this agreement for such child's support, such amounts shall be credited toward this obligation.

Jurisdiction of Court for Modification and Enforcement

The parties agree and consent that the Superior Court of _____ County
shall retain jurisdiction for the purpose of resolving any disputes concerning
the enforcement, modification, or interpretation of this agreement for a
period of _____ years. Any such application to the court shall be made
pursuant to applicable court rules and the civil practice act. This provision
is complementary to the provisions hereinafter made for mediation under
the rules of the Family Mediation Association.

Representation as to Husband's Income

Husband's adjusted gross income for the year 1978 was approximately
$26,000 before payment of income taxes and other required deductions, and
it is projected that the husband will have adjusted gross income for the year
1979 in the approximate amount of $28,000 before deductions. Payments
for the support and maintenance of wife and children herein set forth are
premised on the foregoing.

Representation as to Wife's Income

Wife's adjusted gross income for the year 1978 was approximately $9000
before payment of income taxes and other required deductions, and it is
projected that the wife will have adjusted gross income for the year 1979 in
the approximate amount of $10,000 before deductions. Payments for the
support and maintenance of wife and children herein set forth are premised
on the foregoing.

Modification of Agreement

A. Nothing contained in this agreement shall be deemed to preclude husband or wife from time to time and at any time, to apply to a court of competent jurisdiction for a modification, upward or downward, of the foregoing support provisions, upon the grounds that needs or financial circumstances of the husband, the wife, or a minor child require such
modification.

B. Notwithstanding anything to the contrary contained in this agreement, or in any order of a court of competent jurisdiction based upon this
agreement, parties further agree as follows:

1. The obligations under this agreement of husband for support and for

the future payment of any additional sums of money provided for in this agreement are upon the condition that the husband and wife shall continue to be employed and continue to receive earnings as herein represented which are presently sufficient to meet their obligations under this agreement as well as to support and maintain themselves and meet their other obligations.

2. In the event that the amount of husband's or wife's earnings from employment shall be substantially reduced, or terminate, then husband or wife shall have the right to apply to a court of competent jurisdiction to modify the support provisions contained in this agreement, or the provisions of any order of a court of competent jurisdiction based on this agreement.

3. The court shall be authorized to make any modification retroactive to the date of the event which supports the need for modification. It is further specifically agreed that any failure by husband to have fully paid all accrued support payments at the time said matter comes before the court, shall not place husband in contempt nor otherwise prejudice his right to seek a modification of his support obligation. In any modification hearing, whether brought by husband or wife, the court shall take into account all financial and other relevant circumstances of both the wife and the husband.

Alimony—Waiver by Reason of Common-Law Relationship

In the event that the wife ever at any time or place lives or resides in or occupies the same residence or quarters with any man in such manner as to cause others in the same community to believe that she is the wife of that man or that he is her husband, she shall be deemed to have remarried even though no marriage ceremony has ever been performed between her and such man. Upon the happening of such event, the husband's obligations to pay the wife any further alimony shall terminate in the same manner as if a ceremonial marriage had taken place. It is further provided that the wife shall be entitled upon such event to receive increased alimony payments, if any are provided for in this agreement, in the event of her ceremonial marriage. Her acceptance of such payment shall be conclusive evidence of her remarriage within the meaning of that term as used in this agreement.

Dependents' Exemption for Income Tax Purposes

The parties hereto hereby expressly agree that so long as the husband makes the payments herein called for to be paid to the wife and the children as the same fall due and complies with his other obligations hereunder, including the maintenance of insurance for the benefit of the children, the _____ shall have the sole and exclusive right to claim the children as his/her dependents for income tax purposes with both federal and state governments, and the _____ agrees that he/she will not claim said children as exemptions. (*Comment:* In some instances, the exemptions may be split between husband and wife so she can receive head-of-household tax treatment.)

Tax Assessments—Hold Harmless Agreement

The husband shall and does hold the wife harmless from any and all assessments of income taxes imposed by all state and federal governments during the entire term of the marriage as set forth herein up to and including the taxable year 197__, and agrees to pay any and all deficiencies which may be assessed, and assumes all responsibility for the filing of the returns and failure to file any returns and the accuracy of said returns. Husband agrees to indemnify and hold the wife harmless from any and all assessments or losses of every kind, character, and description by any taxing authority during such period. The husband shall defend all attempts to impose any assessment or collect the same against the wife or against any property of the wife, including that conveyed or transferred herein, at his sole cost and expense and shall take any and all legal and other actions necessary to protect all property belonging to the wife. Should the husband fail to perform any of his obligations hereunder, the wife shall be entitled to recover from the husband any and all losses or assessments together with all expenses, including reasonable attorney's fees. [*Comment:* This is the usual provision found in separation agreements. The wife's division of marital property may be such as would suggest sharing this contingent liability.]

Mutual Release

Except as otherwise expressly provided herein, the parties shall and do mutually remise, release, and forever discharge each other from any and all actions, suits, debts, claims, demands, and obligations whatsoever, in both law and equity, which each of them ever had, now has, or may hereafter have against the other, which accrued up to the date of the execution of this agreement. Each party hereby releases and relinquishes any and all rights he or she may hereafter acquire as spouse under the present or future laws of any jurisdiction to share in the estate of the other party upon the latter's death, except as herein set forth, and to act as executor or administrator of the other party's estate. This provision is intended to constitute a mutual waiver by the parties to take against each other's last wills, except as herein provided under the present or future laws of any jurisdiction whatever.

Modifications and Waivers

Except as specifically provided herein, no modification or waiver of any of the terms hereof shall be valid unless in writing and signed by both of the parties. No waiver of any breach hereof or default hereunder shall be deemed a waiver of any subsequent breach or default of the same or similar nature.

Not Agreement for Divorce—Nonmerger

This agreement is made without in any manner consenting to a divorce between the parties, but nothing contained herein shall be construed to bar or prevent either party from suing for absolute divorce in any court of competent jurisdiction upon grounds afforded by such jurisdiction. This agreement shall be offered in evidence in such action and, if acceptable to the court, shall be incorporated by reference into any decree which may be granted between the parties hereto. Notwithstanding such incorporation, this agreement shall not be merged into any decree, but shall survive independently of such final judgment and decree.

Voluntary Execution

The parties acknowledge that they are entering into this agreement freely and voluntarily; that they have ascertained and weighed all the facts and circumstances likely to influence their judgment herein; that they have sought and obtained legal advice from the impartial advisory attorney who has drafted this settlement agreement at their joint instance and request. In selecting said attorney to advise them, they have been free to select any attorney of their choice. They have been duly appraised of their respective legal rights and all the provisions hereof. All legal questions pertinent hereto have been fully and satisfactorily explained to them. They have given due consideration to such provisions and questions, and they clearly understand and assent to all the provisions hereof.

Attorney's Fees to Prevailing Party

If any action is brought to modify or enforce any of the provisions of this agreement, or of any order or judgment embodying its provisions, the prevailing party shall be awarded reasonable attorney's fees and costs, but in no case exceeding the sum of $_____.

Mediation

In the event of any future controversy arising out of or relating to this contract or the breach thereof, either prior to or after its incorporation into a final decree of divorce, the parties agree that the controversy shall be resolved in accordance with the Marital Mediation Rules of the Family Mediation Association. The arbitration of any impasse reached during mediation shall be in accordance with the Marital Arbitration Rules of the Family Mediation Association in accordance with the Statutory Arbitration Laws of the State of *Georgia (Georgia Code Title VII, Chapter 2). The parties further agree that such controversy shall be submitted to three arbitrators, one of whom shall be chosen by each of the parties and one by the arbitrators chosen by the parties, which arbitrators shall be selected from the panel of arbitrators of the Family Mediation Association pursuant to its rules.* (Italic wording is to be in conformity with local state law.) The parties further agree that they will faithfully observe this agreement and the rules under which said mediation and arbitration are conducted, and that the award rendered by the arbitrators shall be final and binding upon them, and may be entered in and made the judgment of any court having jurisdiction.

Entire Agreement

Neither party has been induced to execute and deliver this agreement by reason of any representation or promise by or on behalf of the other party not herein contained. Neither party shall assert or claim that this agreement or any provision thereof is invalid by reason of any such representation or promise. The parties have incorporated in this agreement their entire understanding. They are not relying on any representations other than those expressly set forth herein.

IN WITNESS WHEREOF, the parties have hereunto set their hands and affixed their seals to three counterparts of this agreement, each of which shall constitute an original, this the _____ day of _____, 197__.

_____ (Seal)
Husband

_____ (Seal)
Wife

Signed in the presence of

_____

Mediator

_____

Advisory Attorney

Concurrence (Nonconcurrence) of Mediator

The general provisions contained in the foregoing agreement were reached by the parties in mediation conducted by the undersigned mediator, under the Rules of the Family Mediation Association. Legal advice and services required for drafting this agreement were provided by the Advisory Attorney whose signature appears above.

Having reviewed with the parties all the facts and circumstances leading up to their having reached this agreement, the mediator, as required by the Mediation Rules, now expresses his (concurrence) (nonconcurrence) therewith as evidence that, in the mediator's view, the agreement is fair to each party and provides adequately for their children.

This the _____ day of _____, 197__.

_____

Mediator

Appendix FMA-G
Forms for Use in Marital Mediation

FMA 177

PERSONAL DATA AND INFORMATION

1. Full Name _____

   Home Address _____ Home Phone _____

   Work Address _____ Work Phone _____

   Lived at present address since _____

2. Spouse's Full Name _____

   Spouse's Home Address _____ Home Phone _____

   Work Address _____ Work Phone _____

3. MARRIAGE   Date _____ Place _____

4. CHILDREN:

Full Name	Date of Birth	Living With
_____	_____	_____
_____	_____	_____
_____	_____	_____
_____	_____	_____
_____	_____	_____

5. Are you and your spouse living together now? _____

   If not, state date of separation _____

6. Are you employed? _____ If yes, state:

   Name of Employer _____

   Job Title _____ Nature of Job _____

   _____

   Employed since _____ Salary _____

7. Is your spouse employed ? _____ If yes, state:

   Name of Employer _____

   Job Title _____ Nature of Job _____

   _____

   Employed since _____ Salary _____

8. Date of Birth: Self _____ Spouse _____

9. List all prior marriages of yourself or your spouse. (Include name of prior spouse and how, when, and where prior marriage terminated.)

_____

_____

_____

10. List names and ages of any children of any prior marriage of yourself or your spouse, and state with whom such children live.

_____

_____

_____

11. Have you an interest in reconciliation? _____ Does your spouse, as far as you know? _____.

12. Do you anticipate a dispute about custody of the children? _____

13. Do you have an attorney: Name _____
    Address _____ Phone _____

14. Spouse's attorney: Name _____
    Address _____ Phone _____

15. Do you have a will? _____

16. Are there joint bank accounts to which spouse has access? _____
    If so, specify _____

17. Does your spouse have credit cards for which you are responsible?
    _____. If so, specify: _____

18. Who referred you to us? _____

_____   _____

(date)   Signature

FMA 277

Financial Information and Income Statement

The financial information called for on the following pages is important. If you need help in completing any item, please let your mediator know.

Assets

Estimate the value of each of the following items of property. If any item is located in a jurisdiction other than that in which you live, indicate where such item is located, and, if necessary, give details on a separate sheet. Indicate how much of each asset held in joint ownership was contributed by husband and how much by wife. Attach copies of Federal Income Tax Returns for last three calendar years and copies of all financial statements furnished banks or other creditors during the same period.

	Husband	Wife	Joint
A. Bank Accounts and Savings Accounts:			
	___	___	___
	___	___	___
	___	___	___
	___	___	___
B. Notes, Accounts Receivable (i.e., money owed to you. Indicate by whom payable, amount, and date or dates payable):			
	___	___	___
	___	___	___
	___	___	___
	___	___	___
C. Stocks, Bonds, Mutual Funds:			
	___	___	___
	___	___	___
	___	___	___
	___	___	___
D. Real Estate (Home and other):			
	___	___	___
	___	___	___
	___	___	___
E. Life Insurance — Name of Company, Policy Number, face value, type (i.e., "term," "Ordinary life," etc.) and location of policy:			
	___	___	___
	___	___	___
	___	___	___
	___	___	___
F. Business or Professional Interests (Please furnish last balance sheet and P & L statement, tax return, buy-sell agreements, etc.):			
	___	___	___
	___	___	___
	___	___	___
	___	___	___

G. Miscellaneous Property (Patents, trademarks, copyrights, royalties, employee benefits (please furnish last statement and descriptive booklet), stock options, etc.):

_____   ____ ____ ____
_____   ____ ____ ____
_____   ____ ____ ____
_____   ____ ____ ____

H. Personal Effects, Automobile, Tangible Personal Property:

Total Assets

Liabilities

| | | Owed By | |
| --- | Husband | Wife | Joint |

A. Mortgages on Real Estate:

B. Notes Payable to Banks and Others:

C. Loans on Insurance Policies:

D. Other Debts:

Total Liabilities

Net Worth (Assets minus Liabilities)

Total Liabilities and Net Worth

178

	Husband	Wife

Annual Income

Gross Salary ____ ____
Less:
  Witholding (____) (____)
  FICA (____) (____)
  Other deductions (Itemize):

_____ (____) (____)
_____ (____) (____)
_____ (____) (____)
_____ (____) (____)

Net Salary ____ ____
Dividend Income* ____ ____
Interest Income* ____ ____
Income from Trusts* ____ ____
Rental Income* ____ ____
Other Income (specify)*_____ ____ ____
_____ ____ ____
_____ ____ ____
Anticipated Support Payments ____ ____
         Total Annual Income ____ ____

Less deductions for:
  Estimated Taxes (____) (____)
  Self-Employment Taxes (____) (____)
  Other Deductions for Tax Payments on Income
    Not Subject to Withholding (____) (____)
         Total Deductions (____) (____)
      Net Annual (take home) Income ____ ____
  Average Monthly Net (take home) Income
      (1/12th of Annual Figure) ____ ____

*If this income is received jointly, so indicate (✔) and divide between husband and wife.

FMA 377

Monthly Expense Budget

If you do not anticipate that the children of your present marriage will be living with you, complete only column A. If you anticipate that the children will be living with you, please attempt to distribute your estimated monthly needs between columns A and B. Some will be difficult, such as rent. On rent, for example, you may estimate what a residence for yourself alone would cost and list that cost in column A, then estimate the cost for yourself and the children, and list in column B the difference between that cost and the amount listed in column A. If you have questions about the distribution, please ask your mediator about it. The numbers in parentheses correspond to columns on "Analysis of Family Expenditures" Sheet.

ITEMS		A (Yourself)	B (Children)
Set-Asides:			
Emergencies and Future Goals (from Schedule A)	(1)	_____	_____
Seasonal Expenses (from Schedule B)	(2)	_____	_____
Regular Monthly Expenses:			
Housing Rent	(3)	_____	_____
House Payments			
Principal and Interest	(3)	_____	_____
Real Estate Taxes	(3)	_____	_____
Home Insurance	(3)	_____	_____
Other (specify) _____	(3)	_____	_____
Utilities:			
Electricity	(4)	_____	_____
Gas/Heating Oil	(5)	_____	_____
Telephone	(6)	_____	_____
Water	(7)	_____	_____
Other (specify) _____		_____	_____
Installment Debt Payments (from Schedule C)	(8)	_____	_____
Total of Above		_____	_____
Day-to-Day Expenses:			
Food and Dairy: At home	(9)	_____	_____
Away from home	(9)	_____	_____
Clothing (including working clothes)	(10)	_____	_____

	A (Yourself)	B (Children)

Transportation:

  Gas and Oil   (11) _____ _____

  Auto Repair & Maintenance   (11) _____ _____

  Other (bus, taxi, parking, etc.)   (11) _____ _____

Health, Medical, and Dental:

  Medical, Dental & Hospital Insurance   (12) _____ _____

  Medical & Health Care (not covered by insurance)   (12) _____ _____

  Dental (not covered by insurance)   (12) _____ _____

  Medicines & Drugs   (12) _____ _____

Household Operation & Maintenance:

  Repairs   (13) _____ _____

  Garden or Yard Work   (13) _____ _____

  Replacement of furnishings   (13) _____ _____

  Dry Cleaning & Laundry   (13) _____ _____

  Domestic Help (_____ days at $_____ per day)   (13) _____ _____

  Children's Day Care   (13) _____ _____

  Other (specify) _____   (13) _____ _____

Education, Self and Children (Immediate Needs)

  Private School Tuition   (14) _____ _____

  College Tuition   (14) _____ _____

  Books and Fees   (14) _____ _____

  Other (specify) _____   (14) _____ _____

Variable Monthly Expenses:

  Drug/Variety Store Items   (15) _____ _____

  Books, Magazines, Newspapers   (15) _____ _____

  Children's Allowances   (15) _____ _____

  Charities, Gifts, Contributions   (15) _____ _____

  Dues (Club or Professional not included as business expenses)   (15) _____ _____

  Cultural/Recreational   (15) _____ _____

  Other (specify) _____   (16) _____ _____

  _____   (17) _____ _____

  _____   (18) _____ _____

           Total Monthly Expenses   _____ _____

FMA 377A

Emergencies and Future Goals

Schedule A

Type of Fund	Probable Cost	Date Desired	Amount to set aside this year	Amount to set aside per month
Emergency				
Savings				
Major Appliances and Equipment				
Home Improvement, Painting, Major Repair				
Education Self Children				
Auto Replacement				
Debt Retirement (other than installment)				
Investment				
Other (specify):				
TOTALS	$	XXX	$	$

FMA 377B

Seasonal Expenses

Schedule B

Expense	Date Needed	Amount	
		Per Year	Per Month
Taxes (Auto Tags, Ad Valorum)			
Auto Insurance			
Life & Disability Insurance			
Vacation			
Other (specify):			
TOTALS	XXX	$	$

FMA 377C

Installment Debt Payments

Schedule C

Name of Creditor	Balance Owed*	Amount of Monthly Payment	Date of Last Payment	Due Date of Next Payment**
Total Balance and Monthly Payments				
Total Delinquent Payments				

* Payment times remaining number of payments.

** If payments are delinquent, due date of next payment may be earlier than current date or even the date of last payment.

ANALYSIS OF FAMILY EXPENDITURES

YEAR AND MONTH	Set-Asides		Regular Monthly Expenses							Day-to-Day Expenses						Variable Monthly Expenses			
	Emergencies & Future Goals	Seasonal Expenses	Housing	Utilities				Installment Debt		Food & Dairy	Clothing	Transportation	Medical & Dental	Household Operation	Education	Incidentals			
				Electric	Gas & Oil	Phone	Water												
	1	2	3	4	5	6	7	8		9	10	11	12	13	14	15	16	17	18

FMA 577

Predivorce Mediation-Arbitration Agreement

STATE OF_____
COUNTY OF_____

This agreement is made between the undersigned husband and the undersigned wife, hereinafter referred to together as "the parties" and the _____ (name of mediation service).

WITNESSETH:

That the parties are now living separately or have reached a decision to do so as a result of unreconciled differences which make their continuing to live together as man and wife intolerable until and unless such differences are resolved; and/or

That either one or both of the parties have reached a decision to dissolve their marriage or that they are seriously considering this alternative; and

That in connection with living separately and the possible dissolution of their marriage, they are desirous of reaching settlement through mediation and/or arbitration of one or more of the following matters: division of property, custody of minor children, child support, spousal maintenance, cost of mediation and arbitration, and attorneys fees; and

That this agreement is made in consideration of the parties' desire to reach settlement of existing controversies between them, under the Marital Mediation Rules of the Family Mediation Association, which might otherwise be the subject of litigation; and

That the signing of this agreement shall be evidence of each party's sincere intention to avoid for himself, for the other party, and for their children, if any, the anxiety, frustration, and bitterness that often arises between parties in connection with the above controversies;

NOW, THEREFORE, in consideration of the above, the parties further contract and agree:

1. Mediation shall be conducted by _____ mediator(s) who shall be compensated at the rate of $_____ per hour for hours spent in the conduct of mediation sessions.

2. An advisory attorney shall be appointed, subject to approval by the parties, to provide legal advice during the mediation process and draft the settlement contract reached between the parties, which contract shall provide for arbitration of any unresolved controversies. The advisory attorney shall be compensated at the rate of $_____ per hour for time spent in mediation sessions, and at the same rate per hour for time authorized by the parties for legal research and drafting the contract of settlement.

3. The parties acknowledge that they have read and had full opportunity to have explained to them the Marital Mediation Rules of the Family Mediation Association, a copy of which has been furnished to each party and is made a part of this agreement. The parties further contract and agree that they will faithfully abide by all the rules during the mediation process, and in the event any part of the controversies existing between them is unresolved when mediation is terminated, such controversies shall be submitted to arbitration under said rules.

IN WITNESS WHEREOF, this agreement is signed by the parties and the _____
(name of mediation service) this the _____ day of _____ , 19_____ .

_____   _____
Husband   *Wife*

                                                                      _____
                                                                      *(name of mediation
                                                                       service)*

                                                                      by

                                                                      _____

FMA 677

Postdivorce Mediation-Arbitration Agreement

STATE OF_____
COUNTY OF_____

This agreement is made between the undersigned who were formerly husband and wife, hereinafter referred to together as "parties," and the _____ (name of mediation service).

WITNESSETH:

That the parties were divorced on the _____ day of _____ , 19_____ , under the provisions of a final judgment and decree of _____ (name and location of court) a copy of which is attached hereto, and to which reference is hereby made; and

That a controversy exists between the parties regarding the provisions made in said judgment and decree relating to one or more of the following matters: division of marital property, spousal maintenance (alimony), support of the minor children of the parties, custody of the minor children, and visitation rights, to wit:

(Here specifically describe each matter in controversy, indicating the position of each party. Add supplemental pages if necessary.)

That this agreement is made in consideration of the parties' desire to reach settlement of the above described controversies under the Marital Mediation Rules of the Family Mediation Association, and avoid having these controversies become the subject of litigation; and

That when the aforesaid controversies have been resolved by mediation and/or arbitration as provided for in this agreement, the aforesaid judgment and decree may be modified in accordance therewith at the instance of either party by consent order of court; and

That the signing of this agreement shall be evidence of each party's sincere intention to avoid for himself, for the other party, and for their children, if any, the anxiety, frustration, and bitterness that often arises between parties in connection with the above controversies;

NOW, THEREFORE, in consideration of the above, the parties further contract and agree:

1. That mediation shall be conducted by _____ mediator(s) who shall be compensated at the rate of $_____ per hour for hours spent in the conduct of mediation sessions.

2. _____ is hereby selected by the parties to serve as advisory attorney during the mediation process, and to draft the agreement reached between the parties which shall provide for a consent order to be taken revising the aforesaid judgment and decree. The advisory attorney shall be compensated at the rate of $_____ per hour as authorized by the parties.

3. The parties acknowledge that they have read and had full opportunity to have explained to them the Marital Mediation Rules of the Family Mediation Association, which are incorporated into and made a part of this agreement. The parties further contract and agree that they will faithfully abide by all the rules and that, in the event any part of the

controversies is unresolved when mediation is terminated, such controversies shall be submitted to arbitration under the Marital Arbitration Rules of the Family Mediation Association and the award of the arbitrator shall be final and binding upon both parties.

IN WITNESS WHEREOF, this agreement is signed by the parties and the _____ (name of mediation service), this the _____ day of _____ , 19_____ .

_____
Husband

_____
Wife

_____
(name of mediation service)

by

_____

FMA 777

Temporary Custody and Maintenance Agreement

STATE OF_____
COUNTY OF_____

 This agreement is made and entered into this the _____ day of _____ 19_____ , between _____ , hereinafter referred to as "husband," and _____ hereinafter referred to as "wife."

WITNESSETH:

That husband and wife have entered into an agreement to settle by mediation and arbitration under the rules of the Family Mediation Association all matters relating to custody of minor children, support of minor children, spousal maintenance, and division of property in connection with a decision of one or both parties to live separately and/or the dissolution of their marriage, and

 That there are _____ minor children which are an issue of their marriage, to wit, ____

_____ , who are hereinafter referred to as "children," and

 That the husband and wife wish to enter into an agreement providing for the temporary custody and temporary support of the children, if any; temporary support of the spouse seeking maintenance; physical possession of certain personal and/or real property; maintenance of the present status of assets except in the usual course of business and provision for payment of the cost of mediation and arbitration.

 NOW, THEREFORE, in consideration of the above, the husband and wife contract and agree as follows:

 1. This agreement shall remain in force and without any further notice or service (which is hereby waived) it may be made a temporary order of a court having jurisdiction upon the application of either party at any time before a final settlement contract has been executed and/or the arbitrator's award has been made a judgment of the court having jurisdiction.

 2. The minor children shall be in the temporary custody of the _____ , and the _____ shall have the right to visit the children and have them visit him/her as follows:

_____
_____
_____

 3. The _____ shall pay to the _____ for the temporary support of the minor children which are in his/her temporary custody the sum of $_____ per _____ beginning on _____ and continuinig thereafter on the same date or dates each month so long as this contract is in force.

 4. The _____ shall pay to the _____ as temporary maintenance for his/her support and the support of _____ the sum of $_____ per _____ beginning on _____ and continuing thereafter on the same date or dates each month so long as this contract is in force.

 5. The _____ shall have the right to possession of the residence presently or previously occupied by the parties, and the _____ shall be responsible for payment of rent or mortgage payments, taxes, and insurance thereon in the amount of $_____ per month so long as this contract is in force or until _____ whichever first occurs and thereafter _____

_____
_____

6. The parties have agreed upon a temporary division of household furnishings and automobiles as follows: _____

_____

_____

_____

7. The parties agree that the cost of mediation, arbitration, and the impartial advisory attorney's services shall be paid by the _____ .

8. This agreement is made under a situation in which the parties are living in a bona fide state of separation and one or both parties have made, or are considering, a decision to dissolve the marriage. This contract shall not be construed as an agreement by either party to seek or obtain a divorce from the other.

9. The parties agree that while this contract is in force, they shall each have the right to live separate and apart from the other and each shall be free from the interference, molestation, authority, and control, direct or indirect, by the other as fully as if sole and unmarried.

10. The parties having reached impasse over certain matters relating to temporary custody and support, the Family Mediation Association is hereby authorized to appoint, under its Marital Mediation Rules, a single, impartial arbitrator under the laws of the state of _____ .

The decision of said arbitrator upon matters submitted to him hereunder shall be final and binding upon both parties, and may be submitted, together with this contract, to a court of competent jurisdiction and made a temporary order of court. The parties hereby submit to said arbitrator for decision the following matters: _____

_____

_____

_____

11. The parties have the following joint assets and charge accounts. No withdrawal or other disposition or change shall be made by either party in any asset except as provided under "additional stipulations." Neither party shall make any further charges under any of the following accounts or any other for which both parties are liable either contractually or legally, except as provided under "additional stipulations."

asset	amount	charge accounts	amount
_____	_____	_____	_____
_____	_____	_____	_____
_____	_____	_____	_____
_____	_____	_____	_____
_____	_____	_____	_____

12. Additional Stipulations _____

_____

_____

_____

_____

Signed in the presence of:

_____

_____
Husband

_____

_____
Wife

FMA 877

Mediator's Record
of Sessions, Charges, And Escrow Deposit

File # _____

Clients' names _____

	Hr. Rate
Mediator #1 _____	
	Hr. Rate
Attorney _____	

Mediator #2 _____

	Hr. Rate
	Hr. Rate

Other _____

Atty. telephone _____ Client Phones   wife _____

husband _____

Mediation deposit collected from _____

_____

Date	Session #	Mediator #1 Hours	Mediator #2 Hours	Attorney Hours	Other Hours	Charges	Escrow Deposits	Escrow Balance	Remarks

FMA 977

Agreement for Representation

STATE OF_____
COUNTY OF_____

This agreement is made between the undersigned husband and the undersigned wife, hereinafter referred to together as "the parties," and the undersigned attorney at law.

WITNESSETH:

That the parties have reached a decision to dissolve their marriage and are now living in a state of separation; and

That one or both parties considers the marriage to be irretrievably broken without there being any likelihood that they may become reconciled; and

That the parties through mediation have entered into a written settlement agreement resolving all issues of property division, spousal maintenance, child support, custody of minor children, and attorney's fees.

NOW, THEREFORE, in consideration of the above, the parties contract and agree:

1. The undersigned attorney may represent the _____ for the purpose of obtaining an uncontested divorce upon the ground that the marriage is irretrievably broken and provided the settlement agreement reached between the parties is included in the final judgment and decree.

2. The fee charged by the attorney shall be $_____ plus court costs not exceeding $_____ .

3. In the event any controversy should arise between the parties subsequent to this contract and prior to the granting of a final decree of divorce, or if for any reason it should appear that the settlement agreement reached by the parties in mediation will not be included in the decree as contemplated herein, the attorney shall proceed no further with the representation of the _____ and will withdraw so as to allow one or both parties to employ other counsel of their choice.

4. Upon such withdrawal, the attorney shall make a reasonable adjustment in which any unearned portion of prepaid fees is refunded.

5. Written notice delivered to the attorney's office from either party indicating that a controversy has arisen shall require the attorney's withdrawal as above provided.

6. Upon his withdrawal, the attorney shall so advise each party in writing.

IN WITNESS WHEREOF, this agreement is signed by the parties and the attorney this the _____ day of _____ , 19_____ .

_____
Husband

_____
Wife

_____
Attorney

In the presence of:

_____

FMA 1077

Report of Legal Service Plan

Family Mediation Association[a]

1725D Franciscan Terrace

Winston-Salem, N. C. 27107

phone (919) 788-3964

August 14, 1978

Secretary,
The North Carolina State Bar
Post Office Box 25850
Raleigh, North Carolina 27611

Re: Report of Legal Service Plan

The information furnished in this letter offered under the provisions of Cannon of Ethics 2, DR 2-103 (D) 5 (e).

The Family Mediation Association, Inc. is a Georgia corporation authorized to conduct affairs in the State of North Carolina under a Certificate of Authority issued by the Secretary of State of North Carolina on August 7, 1978. It is incorporated as a non-profit educational and community service organization certified by the Internal Revenue Service as meeting the requirements of Section 501 (c) 3 of the Internal Revenue Code. Contributions to the Association are thus deductable against income for tax purposes.

The primary goals of the Association are research, development of techniques for conflict resolution, stratagies for improving the quality of family life, public education, and professional training. Related to these goals is the delivery of services which are, in part, legal services.

All legal services are performed by licensed members of the North Carolina Bar, who are members of the Association's panel of Impartial Advisory Attorneys, or who have been mutually selected by the parties to serve in this role under the Association's Marital Mediation Rules. Any active member of the bar may make application for membership on the panel and invitations to attorneys will be regularly extended during educational presentations. Attorneys who appear to be especially well qualified may be invited to make application for panel membership. (See application form enclosed)

The association observes the following criteria in the selection of panel members:

1. Good moral character and professional reputation.

2. Evidence of significant training and experience in family law.

---

[a]The Family Mediation Association has its national headquarters at 5018 Allan Road, Washington, D.C.; telephone 301-320-3300.

3. Knowledge of tax implications associated
with marital dissolution.

4. Ability to draft a settlement agreement conforming
to the wishes of the parties that is clear,
comprehensive, and is designed to meet the
post divorce needs of the family.

5. Willingness to attend a training seminar on
the impartial role of the attorney under the
Association's Marital Mediation Rules, and
the Association's standards for drafting
settlement agreements.

6. Willingness to provide an agreed number of hours
of professional time on a low cost or free basis
to clients who are participating in the Association's
research program.

7. Willingness to observe the Association's Marital
Mediation Rules while providing legal services to
clients who have adopted them.

The Association reserves the right to remove the name
of any attorney from its panel, if, in its judgment, such
attorney is not meeting selection standards on a continuing
basis.

When panel attorneys provide legal service to
members or beneficiaries of the Association:

1. The attorney and not the Association is responsible
for the legal advice given. Accordingly, the
Association does not interfere with the attorney's
exercise of legal judgment.

2. The attorney's clients are the Association's
members or beneficiaries. The Association is not
the attorney's client.

3. The Association in no way participates directly
or indirectly in fees paid by clients for legal
services.

Under the provisions of Cannon 2, DR 2-103, EC 2-7,
EC 2-10, and EC 2-15 the Association proposes to offer lawyer
referral service which will be limited to its field of interest
in family law under the following conditions:

1. The attorney to whom clients are referred must
meet requirements for membership on its panel of
attorneys as above stated.

2. Listing is requested by the attorney.

3. No charge will be made to the attorney for listing.

4. Referrals will be made on the basis of complete information furnished by the attorney regarding fee charges to be made for services rendered.

5. Referrals will be made only to members of the Association.

6. The association will not participate in fees charged by the attorney nor charge the attorney for referrals made.

Members of the panel of attorneys may be invited to participate in public educational programs related to the Association's interest in the family. Portions of these programs will be aimed toward educating the layman in the recognition of legal problems and to heighten his awareness of services available for their solution. These programs will conform to Ethical Considerations, EC 2-1, EC 2-2, EC 2-3, EC 2-4, and EC 2-5.

The Association, in drawing attention to certain provisions of the Code of Professional Responsibility, is not unmindful that the whole CPR is applicable to the conduct of its panel attorneys and to those portions of its activities that relate to the rendition of legal services.

It is the Association's understanding that no action on the part of the State Bar of North Carolina is required other than to place the foregoing information on file. Any further information regarding any of the foregoing activities of the Association will be gladly furnished. Acknowledgement of receipt will be appreciated.

The Association welcomes inquiry from the public and the legal profession regarding its activities and policies. One of its more important functions is to serve as a bridge between the legal and behavioral science professions. In North Carolina as elsewhere the Association looks forward to the continued good relationship and support it has received from members of both professions.

Sincerely,

O. J. Coogler, JD, President
Family Mediation Association, Inc.

OJC:bh
Enclosures:
Application for Membership on Attorney's Panel
Marital Mediation Rules

FMA 1177

General Instructions and Information
for Impartial Advisory Attorneys
(for Georgia attorneys)

The Family Mediation Association, Inc., was chartered on December 27, 1974. Under its charter, its operations are limited to that of a nonprofit educational and research organization, contributions to which are deductible against income under the provisions of the Internal Revenue Code. FMA has received certification from the Internal Revenue Service that contributions to it are deductible.

Under the Code of Professional Responsibility which became effective January 1, 1977, FMA has duly reported its legal service plans to the State Disciplinary Board of the State Bar of Georgia in compliance with Canons of Ethics, Part III(i), DR 2-103, (d)5(9)(c)(7). It has been FMA's continuing goal to work cooperatively with the legal profession for the development of new and innovative techniques for dealing with family distress related to divorce.

Among the goals stated in FMA's charter are the following:

1. To foster the stability of family life by teaching families problem-solving techniques and providing services for resolving disputes.
2. To conduct research in the general field of family and marital dispute resolution
3. To develop and adapt techniques, such as conciliation, mediation, and arbitration for their use in the settlement of family and marital disputes
4. To educate the general public as to alternatives available for family and marital dispute resolution
5. To provide training related to the work of FMA for professionals in the legal, mental health, and other related fields
6. To provide individual and group counseling services related to the work of the association
7. To make services and facilities of the association available to all socioeconomic groups on a basis related to ability to pay or without charge to the extent funds are available for such purposes

The technique of structured mediation, as defined by FMA's Marital Mediation Rules, has been developed and used successfully during the last 3 years. FMA during the same period has offered training courses for attorneys in marital mediation and has presented its system of marital mediation many times to professional groups in Atlanta and around the country. The techniques used in marital mediation have been studied by researchers at Columbia University in New York. As a result of this study, Columbia University is now planning a more in-depth program of study and development of structured mediation as originated by FMA. The Robert Sterling Clark Foundation of New York has funded a grant to further develop FMA's techniques through the Graduate School of Social Work at the University of Georgia in Athens. The mediation experience as reported to us by both clients and researchers is overwhelmingly favorable. When lawyers have referred clients to FMA for marital settlement, the results have reflected favorably upon both the attorney and FMA. While FMA's rate of success in working with couples has far exceeded initial expectations, some couples have come to recognize that divorce is simply not economically feasible for the family and have thus discontinued mediation. Others may reach impasse in mediation, so that arbitration becomes necessary. While no doubt these results were contrary to client expectations, we do not regard them as failures either of the system or with regard to outcome.

On the basis of a survey made of over 300 cases selected at random from the Fulton County Court records, it is clear that the level of service rendered to clients through FMA would lie within at least the upper 10 percentile as to quality and thoroughness. This also appears to be true in other parts of the country, judging by a study made at Yale University School of Law, reported in the November 1976 issue of the *Yale Law Journal*. According to this research, 79 percent of attorney's clients who were surveyed reported that they were provided with no tax advice in uncontested divorce cases in which an average charge of $500 was made. FMA, then, while providing a high quality of service, also provides a psychological setting in which the most advanced techniques of interpersonal communications and conflict resolution are employed. The couple is helped in reaching settlement of the four issues which must be dealt with in all settlement agreements:

1. Division of marital property
2. Spousal maintenance (or alimony)
3. Child support
4. Child custody

FMA strongly recommends that each attorney who serves as an advisory attorney avail himself of the opportunity of receiving training at an FMA seminar so that he may more effectively and comfortably function in an impartial role.

The traditional role of the practicing attorney is that of an advocate. He is the champion of his client. His duty is to represent his client zealously. Yet when he is called upon to serve as a judge on the bench or as an impartial arbitrator, attorneys have the demonstrated ability to change roles and become "impartial" as between the parties. Thus assuming the role of impartial advisory attorney is well within the tradition of the profession.

Lawyers who have attempted to serve informally in an impartial role in matrimonial matters have often had cause to regret their well-intentioned effort. Some have found themselves before disciplinary boards, and others have found themselves named as defendants in malpractice actions. FMA's carefully designed procedures, when followed, will avoid these unpleasant outcomes.

FMA's Marital Mediation Rules provide a structure. They call for services of an administrator, an advisory attorney, and a skilled marital mediator, each having explicit responsibilities and guidelines to follow. This is in sharp contrast with any informal arrangement an attorney might work out with divorcing clients.

On August 1, 1977, FMA discontinued providing mediation services in Atlanta and began the development of mediation service delivery through public and private facilities certified by FMA as qualified to provide mediation under its rules. FMA will continue its work in family research, improvement of the mediation process, training of mediators, certification of mediation facilities, and supervision of certified facilities.

FMA's rules and techniques have been adapted and used in various parts of the United States. If you are considering referring your clients for mediation, be sure to ask whether the agency offering the service is certified by FMA. You may confirm this by checking with FMA. If you should wish to refer clients to a certified FMA mediation center, the following steps must be taken:

1. A tax-deductible membership donation must be made by the clients to FMA. The amount of this donation is shown on the fee schedule provided by the center.
2. The clients must have the Marital Mediation Rules carefully explained to them, section by section. An FMA-trained staff person will provide this.

3. If after reading the Marital Mediation Rules and having them explained the couple decides they wish to reach settlement under the rules, then they may enter into a Mediation-Arbitration Agreement, under which they adopt the rules and in which the applicable fees are stated.

4. A deposit must be made with the mediation center in the amount agreed upon from the applicable fee schedule in advance of the first mediation session.

5. At the first mediation session, the couple will be asked to enter into a Temporary Settlement Agreement, which will stabilize their financial and custodial arrangements for minor children during the time they are negotiating settlement.

6. When the couple has reached substantial agreement, the mediator will contact you for an appointment which will be attended by both parties and the mediator. The agreement reached during mediation will be outlined, and from this you, as advisory attorney, can develop the formal settlement agreement.

   Option: If your practice does not include a substantial amount of domestic relations work, or for other reasons you would prefer not to draft the settlement agreement, it can be drafted by one of the well-qualified impartial advisory attorneys on FMA's panel. In this instance, the completed contract will be brought to you for your final examination and supervision of its execution by your clients.

7. Following execution of the settlement agreement, most clients will expect that one or the other will then proceed with application for a divorce. If you should wish to handle this procedure on behalf of one of your clients, we recommend that you do so, provided the clients are willing to execute an employment agreement under which you would have the right and duty to withdraw in the event any controversy should arise in connection with the matter, or in the event the settlement agreement is for any reason not to be incorporated in the final judgment and decree. (FMA has designed an acceptable form for this purpose.)

   Option: If you prefer not to handle the divorce action, the center will refer your clients, at your request, to an attorney who will handle the uncontested divorce for them on a nominal-cost basis previously agreed to by the clients.

8. Finally, fee arrangements for all services performed by you as impartial advisory attorney or otherwise for your clients are for negotiation directly between yourself and your clients.

For your general guidance, please note the following:

1. Read the Marital Mediation Rules until you are thoroughly familiar with them. Even though your clients will receive a careful explanation of the rules by an FMA-trained staff person, they may still have questions they wish to ask you and would legitimately have the right to expect that you are familiar with the rules. Please pay particular attention to provisions relating to advisory attorneys.

2. Since arbitration of impasses has been such a rare experience, this outline of procedure has not dealt with the steps to be followed in the event arbitration should become necessary. In such an event, full consultation regarding the steps required will be available to you from the center or FMA. Even though it is unlikely that arbitration will be necessary, we nevertheless suggest that you read the Marital Arbitration Rules so that you will be generally familiar with them.

3. Please observe that the guidelines which the clients agree to follow by adopting the Marital Mediation Rules differ from provisions of local state law. While the clients will have it explained to them that there are differences between the guidelines and local state law, you may consider it advisable to touch upon these issues yourself in advising them to follow mediation as a means of reaching settlement. In this connection please refer to Section 30, relating to marital property; Section 31, relating to spousal maintenance; Section 32, relating to child support; Sections 33 to 37 relating to custody.

These guidelines are a composite resulting from a study of some fifteen states that have adopted marriage and divorce laws patterned after the Uniform Marriage and Divorce Act developed by the Commissioners on Uniform State Laws. Guidelines are provided so that the couple will have something considerably more definitive than is afforded by most state laws. FMA will update its Marital Mediation Rules from time to time so as to provide the most ideal setting in which couples may reach settlement.

4. Do not hesitate to call FMA for any clarification or further information you need so that the Marital Mediation Rules may be followed consistently by all who use them.

5. While FMA does insist that the Marital Mediation Rules be carefully followed, this in no way interfers with the advisory attorney's free exercise of professional judgment in giving legal advice to the clients and assuming responsibility therefor. While all attorneys with whom FMA has worked have been more than willing to follow the mediation rules, FMA does reserve the right to withdraw from further participation with an attorney who does not observe the Marital Mediation Rules.

We are confident that both you and your clients will be well pleased with this collaborative arrangement affording to the client your legal expertise and FMA's skills in facilitating conflict resolution leading to an amicable settlement. Such results will bring to you the sincere appreciation of your clients, and you will have the satisfaction of having participated in a settlement arrangement which is most likely to provide a healthy environment for your client's children.

FMA 1277

APPLICATION FOR MEMBERSHIP ON PANEL OF APPROVED ATTORNEYS

1. _____   _____

last name *first name or initials* *date*

_____

street address *city* *state* *zip code*

2. _____

firm *bus. phone* *res. phone*

3. _____

professional memberships

4. _____

admission to bar (give dates and states of admission)

5. _____

graduate and undergraduate degrees earned (give dates and college or university)

6. _____

professional liability insurance (give name of company and coverage)

*7. Describe the type of practice you have engaged in since admission to the bar or during the last ten years. Indicate the proportion of time devoted to domestic relations practice.

_____

_____

8. Of domestic relations cases you have handled, indicate approximately what proportion or percentage of cases fall into the following categories:

a. You represented ( ) husbands, ( ) wives

b. ( ) Opposing party was not represented by counsel.

c. Settled within ( ) 3 months, ( ) 6 months, ( ) 1 year, ( ) over 1 year.

d. ( ) Settlement reached after opposing counsel claimed to have substantially completed trial preparation.

e. ( ) Settlement reached after you had substantially completed trial preparation.

f. ( ) Settled after case reached jury trial calendar.

g. ( ) Cases tried or settled after selection of jury.

9. Please indicate your usual charges for domestic relations cases as follows:

a. Retainer fee $ _____.

b. Uncontested case with "simple" settlement agreement prepared $_____.

c. Average amount of fees charged $_____.

10. As a member of the panel of attorneys of the Family Mediation Association:

    a. Are you willing to donate 10 or more hours of free professional time per year? ( ) yes ( ) no

    b. Are you willing to give 10 or more additional hours of professional time per year at an hourly rate of $__ per hour? ( ) yes ( ) no

    c. Your hourly rate of charge for other professional time may be quoted at $_____ until further notice to the Association.

       If variable, explain:_____

    d. Are you willing to attend at least one half-day training workshop per year conducted for panel members at a cost not exceeding $_____ ( ) yes ( ) no

*11. Have you ever been arrested for other than a minor traffic offense? ( ) yes ( ) no

    If yes, give details and dates _____

    _____

*12. Have you ever been required to appear before a professional disciplinary commitee? ( ) yes ( ) no

    If yes, give details and dates _____

    _____

13. a. Marital status: ( ) married ( ) single ( ) divorced ( ) widower (If more than once, indicate number of times.)

    b. Children (number, age, and sex) _____

    _____

*14. State briefly what changes, if any, in domestic relations laws you would recommend.

    _____

15. Are you generally in accord with the Association's system of mediation and arbitration of marital and family disputes as it has been developed up to this time, and will you notify the Association in the event of any future change of your position? ( ) yes ( ) no

16. When called upon to perform service as an attorney panel member you accept the obligations provided for advisory attorneys in the Marital Mediation Rules and the Marital Arbitration Rules. Your signature on this application certifies that you have read and understood the Rules and agree to abide by them.

_____
signature of applicant

*Attach additional pages, if necessary, to complete your answers to these items.

FMA 1377

Release of Audiotaped Data

Structured mediation, developed by the Family Mediation Association, Inc., is a new and innovative system for conflict resolution leading to integrated problem-solving. Wide interest has resulted among professionals in the social science and mental health fields, which have led to requests for research data.

Further research, particularly comparative studies involving other systems, is urgently needed to improve structured mediation and to make it more generally available throughout the country.

The Association, as a nonprofit educational-scientific organization, requests your permission to release audiotape recordings of your mediation sessions as research data, strictly limited to qualified researchers associated with similar nonprofit educational-scientific organizations and institutions. If, by reason of your own association with such institutions, you wish to exclude availability to certain institutions, you may note the names of such institutions below.

In all cases strict confidentiality will be maintained. You will not be identified by name even to researchers. Any proposed publication of direct quotations from taped material even without identification will require your further approval.

Signatures below indicate your agreement for the release of taped material under the stated conditions.

This the _____ day of _____ , 197____

Excepted from release: _____

_____   _____
Husband   Wife

                                        FAMILY MEDIATION ASSOCIATION, INC.
                                        By _____
                                        Title _____

Index

203

About the Author

O.J. Coogler received his undergraduate degree in psychology at the University of Georgia and his JD (Juris Doctor) degree from Emory University in Atlanta, Georgia. He is a licensed attorney who practiced for twenty-five years before retiring to pursue his lifelong interest in psychotherapy.

Coogler was the author of the Marriage and Family Counselors Licensing Act, approved by the Georgia Legislature in 1976, and is a licensed counselor under that act. He has achieved clinical membership in the American Association of Marriage and Family Counselors and the International Transactional Analysis Association.

He has been called the "father of the divorce mediation process." In 1974, he began studies that led to his development of structured mediation. He believes it offers a more effective means of resolving human conflict than the present court system and sees its application to divorce settlement as only one among many situations in which this concept may be employed.